SAINSBURY'S

VEGETARIAN COOKING

CAROLE HANDSLIP

NOTES

1. Standard level spoon measurements are used in all recipes.
1 tablespoon = one 15 ml spoon
1 teaspoon = one 5 ml spoon

2. Both metric and imperial measurements have been given in all recipes. Use one set of measurements only and not a mixture of both.

3. Ovens should be preheated to the specified temperature – if using a fan assisted oven, follow manufacturer's instructions for adjusting the temperature.

4. Eggs should be size 3 unless otherwise stated and free-range if possible

5. Pepper should be freshly ground black pepper unless otherwise stated.

6. Milk should be full-fat unless otherwise stated.

7. Fresh herbs should be used unless otherwise stated. If unavailable use dried herbs as an alternative but halve the quantities stated.

8. All microwave information is based on a 650 watt oven. Follow manufacturer's instructions for an oven with a different wattage.

9. Carbohydrate, fat and fibre are measured in grams for the nutritional information.

Published exclusively for
J Sainsbury plc
Stamford Street, London SE1 9LL
by Cathay Books
Michelin House
81 Fulham Road, London SW3 6RB

First published 1990

ISBN 0 86178 6025

Produced by Mandarin Offset
Printed and Bound in Hong Kong

Contents

INTRODUCTION

TO MANY THE WORD 'VEGETARIAN' SUGGESTS THOSE WHO EAT A FEW CARROTS AND A LETTUCE LEAF, WITH NUTS ON SPECIAL OCCASIONS! NOTHING COULD BE FURTHER FROM THE TRUTH. THE VARIETY OF INGREDIENTS IS ENDLESS, IN TASTE, TEXTURE AND COLOUR.

There are varying degrees of vegetarianism dictated by economic choice, medical advice or religious beliefs. Some people – known as 'lacto-vegetarians' – cut out eating meat, all meat products, fish and poultry. Others do not eat meat and meat products but do allow themselves fish. Vegans follow a strict diet – in addition to meat, fish and poultry, they also refuse all dairy products, eggs, and all ingredients with animal origins, including honey and gelatine.

Vegetarian eating is now viewed with respect since it reflects and puts into practice many of the recommendations that nutritionists advise for healthy eating. A vegetarian diet can quite adequately provide all the nutrients required for a balanced diet, including the ones traditionally supplied by meat and fish.

These are:

Protein which is essential for healthy growth and repair of body cells.

Fats which are needed for energy and warmth and for the absorption of the fat-soluble vitamins, A, D, E and K.

Carbohydrates which are needed for energy and warmth.

Fibre which is vital to keep the digestive system functioning smoothly and healthily.

Vitamins are required for body building and maintenance to assist in the metabolism of other nutrients added to provide resistance to infection and disease.

Minerals which are necessary for the growth, development and maintenance of the body and its organs and the functioning of many bodily processes.

To achieve an adequate diet there must be balance between the three major nutrients – proteins, fats and carbohydrates. Vegetarians will find protein in eggs, vegetables, cheese, milk, grains, pulses, nuts and seeds; fats in cheese, milk and other dairy produce, nuts, vegetable oils, spreads and eggs; carbohydrates in sugars and syrups, fruit and vegetables, cereals, pulses and grains; fibre in grains, cereals, pulses, fruits and vegetables and vitamins and minerals in almost all food but especially in fresh raw fruit and vegetables.

Introducing such foods to replace meat, poultry and fish in the diet is not initially easy and should be done gradually. You could start by substituting beans, lentils, vegetables, nuts, cheese and eggs for meat, poultry and fish. Try eating wholegrain cereals, wholewheat pasta and pulses instead of refined foods. In essence serve plenty of vegetables and fruit at each meal.

Vegetarian cookery can be rich and varied; full of wonderful flavours and textures. It can include such ingredients as fresh vegetables and fruit, nuts, grains, seeds, pulses and many specialities, from the Middle and Far East as well as the more familiar ingredients from Europe. I hope this book will encourage those seeking to explore the possibilities of vegetarian cookery and give fresh ideas to those who are already confirmed vegetarians.

Agar Agar

Agar Agar is a setting agent obtained from several different types of seaweed. It is available either in powder or made form and is used as an alternative to animal gelatine.

Beans

Weight for weight, beans contain more protein than meat, fish or eggs and have roughly double the protein content of cereals. The soya bean has the highest protein content, followed by the aduki bean and chickpea. There are more than 20 different types of edible peas and beans which are all rich in iron, potassium and the B group of vitamins. They are also the richest source of vegetable fibre.

All beans should be soaked before cooking and the soaking water should always be thrown away. They should then be covered with fresh water, boiled rapidly for 10 minutes to destroy any harmful toxins which may be present, and the water discarded again. They are then ready to be cooked for the required length of time as specified on the chart (see page 8).

If you have a freezer it is a good idea to cook at least 500 g (1 lb) dried beans at one time, then freeze them in 125 g (4 oz) or 250 g (8 oz) quantities for use as required.

If you are short of time and you have no frozen beans in stock, the wide variety of canned beans now readily available is extremely useful.

Buckwheat

Buckwheat is also known as 'saracen corn'. It is the

seed of a herbaceous plant and is rich in protein, iron and the entire range of B vitamins. It is available in various forms such as flour, groats or roasted buckwheat called 'kasha'.

Cheese

Most hard cheeses are made with animal rennet but a number of vegetarian cheeses such as Danish blue, vegetarian Cheddar and Mozzarella are now available. Many of the softer cheeses such as full-fat soft cheese, cottage cheese, curd cheese, ricotta, feta and goat's cheese are made without the use of animal rennet. Use these in place of the hard and soft cheeses specified in the recipes if you prefer.

Fromage frais is a soft cheese made from pasteurized skimmed milk sometimes enriched with cream. The flavour varies from slightly acid to rich depending on the amount of cream added and the fat content ranges from almost nil up to 8 per cent. Quark is a fresh curd cheese which again varies in fat content depending on how much cream is added.

Dried fruits

Dried fruits are more concentrated in flavour than their fresh counterparts and are ideal for using in cooking. They are a rich source of fibre, minerals such as iron and calcium and vitamins A, C and several of the B group.

Many dried fruits such as apricots, pears, peaches and apples are preserved with sulphur dioxide to keep their colour. To remove this it is advisable to boil the fruit for 1 minute before use and discard the water. Most other dried fruits are sprayed or dipped in preservative to give them a moist appearance, this can be removed by washing the fruit in hot water. There are now dried fruits available that have not been treated with sulphur or preservatives which you can use whenever possible. Their flavour is very good, but the colour may seem dull.

Grains

Grains or cereals are probably the most important staple food in the world. Wheat, rice, barley, oats, millet, rye and maize are the major food grains and all belong to the large grass family. If eaten whole and unrefined they provide valuable fibre in the diet as well as protein, calcium, iron, phosphorus, potassium and B vitamins.

Lentils

Lentils are one of the oldest crops, cultivated since prehistoric times. They are grown all over the Middle East and India in many varieties, the most common being the green or continental lentils, brown lentils and split red lentils. They do not need to be soaked before use, though it will shorten the cooking time if they are. Split red lentils have been shelled and therefore do not have such a high fibre content.

Nuts and Seeds

Nuts and seeds are a high protein food rich in minerals and vitamins. They have a high fat content which is rich in linoleic acid, a colourless oily essential fatty acid. Their addition to any dish makes it more interesting and nourishing and gives it a wonderful flavour. The flavour is further enhanced by roasting or toasting. They can be added to cakes, biscuits and bread and are a delicious addition to many salads.

Oils and Fats

Oils are one of the essentials of our diet, containing lecithin and vitamins A, E and K. They can be divided into three main kinds: saturated, mono-unsaturated and polyunsaturated.

Animal fats which are solid at room temperature are high in saturated fats. Excessive consumption of these fats is associated with heart disease.

Most vegetable oils are high in polyunsaturated fat, which tends to lower the level of cholesterol in the blood. Oils high in polyunsaturates include safflower, sesame and corn oil. Olive oil is mainly mono-unsaturated which has been regarded as neutral although research is being done in this area.

Cold pressed oil is still extracted in the traditional way with a hydraulic press. It is then filtered and retains all its natural flavour. This method is used for soft seeds such as sesame and sunflower and for olives.

Semi-refined oil requires a greater pressure and high temperatures. The seeds are steamed prior to pressing and the resulting oil has a rich colour and strong smell. Refined oil is produced by a method called solvent extraction, which removes most of the original flavour as well as bleaching and deodorizing the oil. This is the cheapest method and has the highest extraction rate, but preservatives are usually added to prevent the oil going rancid.

SALT
The minerals sodium and potassium need to be kept in balance in our bodies. We obtain as much sodium (salt) as we need from our diet without adding extra flavouring. Eating too much salt disturbs the balance with potassium and may lead to high blood pressure and arthritis among many other disorders.

Eminent authorities are advising a much lower salt intake. The amount of salt needed by an adult is 3 to 4 grams daily in a temperate climate. The average consumption in the UK is about 12 grams a day!

Sea salt is obtained by evaporating sea water in enclosed areas. It has a high iodine content and no additives. Table salt has phosphate of lime and other substances added to keep it free-flowing. Rock salt is usually found in the crystalline state in the ground.

Sesame salt or 'Gomasio' is a good alternative to salt. It can be made by grinding 5 parts roasted sesame seeds with 1 part salt.

SEA VEGETABLES
Seaweed has been beneficial to man for many centuries. The Romans, Greeks and Chinese all used it as a food, medicine and fertilizer.

There are many varieties, the most common being arame, kombu, wakame, dulse and nori. They are an excellent source of vitamin C, essential amino acids and trace elements, especially iodine.

SOY SAUCE
Naturally fermented soy sauce made from soya beans with wheat or barley is known as 'shoyu'. The proprietary soy sauce sometimes contains sugar and other additives.

Soy sauce makes an excellent flavouring for stir-fries, stews, sauces and dressings and as it is quite salty it is unnecessary to add further salt. It is available as both light and dark soy sauce, the lighter one being stronger in flavour.

TAHINI
Tahini is a sesame seed paste widely used in the Middle East. It is especially good for flavouring dips, sauces and dressings and can be used as a binding agent in rissoles and nut roasts.

TOFU
Tofu is soya bean curd, which has a mild flavour. Its high protein content makes it a valuable nutritional substitute for meat, fish and dairy products. It is also rich in iron, calcium and B vitamins.

It is a versatile ingredient that can be stir-fried, deep fried, marinated, added to dressing and sauces and even used in desserts. Smoked tofu is firm tofu which has been smoked over hard woods, usually oak, for anything from 3½ to 6 hours.

YOGURT
Yogurt is a very popular fermented milk product which can be made from cow's, sheep's and goat's milk. It is a natural antibiotic and the acid in it kills many harmful organisms. Live yogurt contains bacteria which act on the milk sugars to provide lactic acid, in the same way as do the digestive juices in the stomach, so it is very easily digested as are all types of yogurt. Yogurts differ in their fat content. While those with cream added may contain as much as 10 per cent fat, low-fat yogurts made from concentrated skimmed milk can have a fat content as small as 0.5 per cent.

Greek strained yogurt is thicker than ordinary yogurt and its smooth texture and sweetness make it an excellent substitute for cream. It is made from either cow's or sheep's milk, the latter having a lower fat content.

TO ROAST NUTS AND SEEDS
The flavour of all nuts and seeds except walnuts and pecan nuts, is enhanced by roasting. To brown sunflower, sesame seeds and pumpkin seeds, place the seeds in a heavy based pan with a tight fitting lid. Shake the pan over a moderate heat for about 1 minute or until the seeds begin to pop and turn a pale gold colour.

To roast nuts place in a single layer on a baking sheet, whole or chopped. Put in a hot oven for about 10 minutes, until golden brown. Alternatively, to toast nuts, place under a moderate grill for 3–4 minutes turning frequently.

BREADCRUMBS
Home-made breadcrumbs are useful to have in store for using in recipes. Drop stale brown or white bread through the feed tube into the bowl of a food processor and process for 5–10 seconds. Put the breadcrumbs into freezerproof bags, seal, label and freeze for future use.

Salad sprouts

Mung beans are the most common type of beans to be sprouted. However 'sprouts' can be grown from all kinds of peas, beans and lentils as well as from alfalfa, fenugreek and cereal grains. Some grow at a much faster rate than others. They are an excellent source of protein, dietary fibre, vitamins, minerals and starch.

To sprout pulses and seeds

Select clean whole seeds and soak in cold water overnight. Drain and place in a salad sprouter. Rinse the seeds twice a day with cold water and leave for 2–5 days to sprout depending upon type.

Sprouts will keep in the refrigerator for up to 1 week in a covered container.

Cooking Time Guide for Pulses

All dried beans should be soaked before cooking and the soaking water should always be discarded. They should then be covered with fresh water, boiled rapidly for 10 minutes, to destroy any harmful toxins that may be present, and the water discarded again. They are then ready to be cooked for the required length of time, see below.

Salt can be added, but only towards the end of the cooking time. If it is added before the skins will toughen and the cooking time will increase.

It is not possible to be exact with cooking times as they depend on the freshness of the beans.

Aduki beans	40–45 minutes
Black beans	1½ hours
Blackeye beans	30–45 minutes
Butter beans	45 minutes
Flageolet beans	1 hour
Haricot beans	1¼–1½ hours
Kidney beans	1¼–1½ hours
Mung beans	30–40 minutes
Pinto beans	50–60 minutes
Chickpeas	1¼ hours
Green lentils	45–50 minutes
Red lentils	20–30 minutes

Vegetable stock

ALWAYS KEEP THE WATER IN WHICH YOU COOK VEGETABLES OR BEANS. THIS WILL MAKE AN ADEQUATE LIGHT STOCK, AND CAN BE USED INSTEAD OF WATER IN THIS STOCK RECIPE. YOU CAN ALSO USE THE WATER FROM SOAKING DRIED MUSHROOMS WHEN YOU NEED A STRONG DARK STOCK

1 tablespoon olive oil
1 large onion, chopped roughly
1 clove garlic, chopped
2 carrots, chopped roughly
2 celery sticks, sliced
small piece of turnip or parsnip, chopped
1 leek, sliced
bouquet garni
1 tablespoon soy sauce
1.75 litres (3 pints) water or vegetable water.

Heat the oil in a large pan and fry the onion and garlic until softened. Add the remaining ingredients and bring to the boil. Cover and cook gently for at least 1 hour. Strain, cool and keep in the refrigerator for up to 4 days or freeze, (see below). You can purée the remaining vegetables and use for a thick soup.

Freezing: is recommended. When cold, store and freeze in 125 ml (¼ pint) and 300 ml (½ pint) quantities in plastic containers or ice-cube trays. This will keep for up to 6 months.

MAKES APPROXIMATELY 1.25 LITRES (2 PINTS)

STUFFING VINE LEAVES

SEE RECIPE ON PAGE 14.

Spooning the filling onto the vine leaf.

Folding the vine leaf over the filling.

Rolling up the vine leaf to make a small parcel.

MAKING FILO FLOWERS

SEE RECIPE ON PAGE 11.

Cutting up the filo pastry.

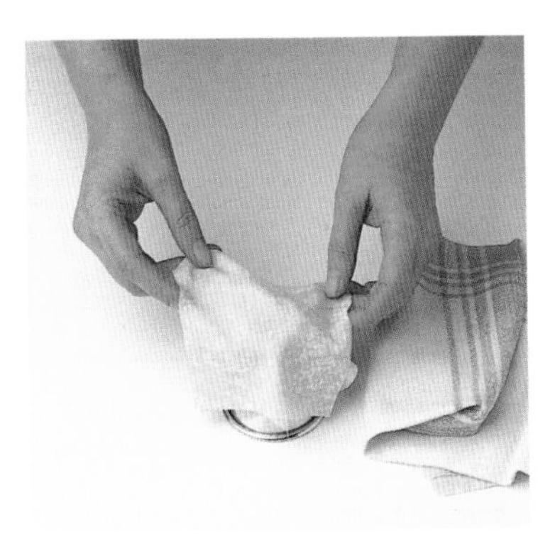

Draping the filo pastry over a dariole mould.

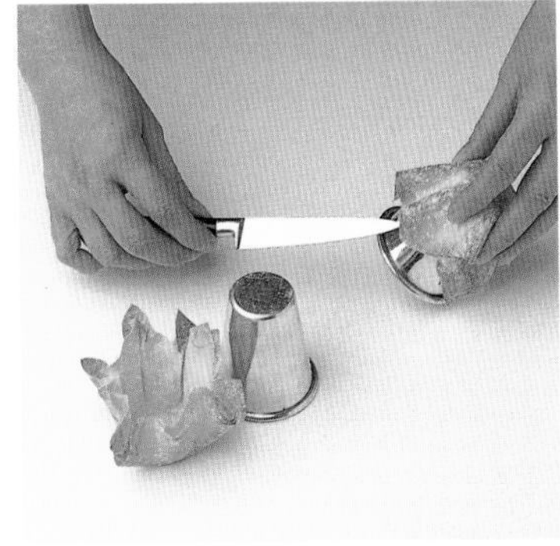

Gently easing the cooked pastry off the dariole mould.

SHAPING BRANDY SNAP BASKETS

SEE RECIPE ON PAGE 83.

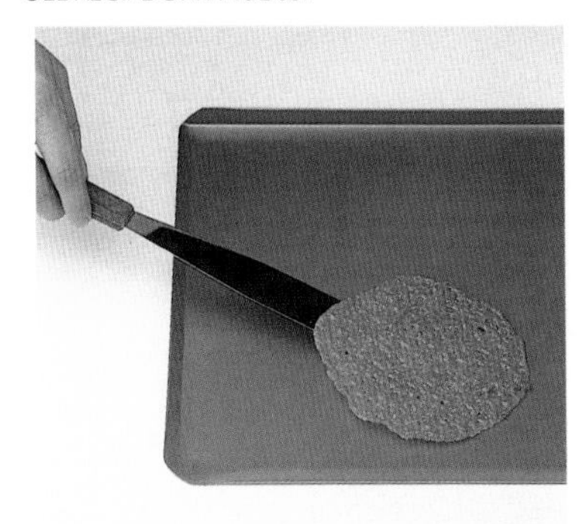

Using a palette knife to remove the brandy snaps from a baking sheet.

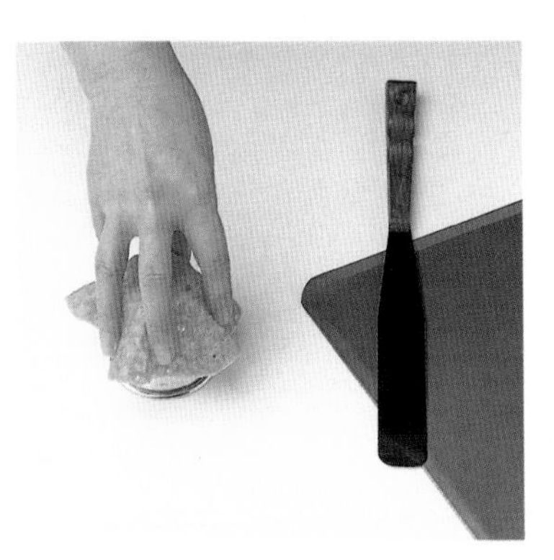

Moulding the brandy snap over a dariole mould.

The finished brandy snap basket.

STARTERS

VEGETARIAN FOOD OFFERS ENDLESS POSSIBILITIES FOR A WIDE VARIETY OF STARTERS. FROM A THICK NOURISHING SOUP TO A LIGHT CONCOCTION OF VEGETABLES IN A DELICATE FILO FLOWER CASE, YOU ARE SURE TO FIND SOMETHING TO SUIT EACH AND EVERY OCCASION.

Filo Flowers

Filo pastry makes a delicate container for this savoury filling and needs no butter spread between the leaves as is normally the case when using this pastry

2 sheets filo pastry
6 quail's eggs
175 g (6 oz) natural fromage frais
1 teaspoon tomato purée
1 clove garlic, crushed
½ teaspoon clear honey
3 tomatoes, skinned, halved and deseeded
1 small avocado, sliced
2 teaspoons chopped basil
salt and pepper
basil sprigs to garnish

Cut the filo pastry into 10 cm (4 inch) squares and stack in a pile. Cover with a cloth to prevent them drying out.

Drape 3 squares of pastry over a dariole mould or glass tumbler, turning each square at a slight angle to the last, and place the mould on a baking sheet. Repeat with the remaining pastry to cover 6 moulds. Bake in a preheated oven, 190°C, 375°F, Gas Mark 5 for 6–8 minutes until golden brown. Leave to cool then gently ease off the moulds with the help of a small knife.

Boil the quail's eggs for 5 minutes then put straight into cold water to cool. Crack the shells and peel very carefully then cut in half.

Mix the fromage frais with the tomato purée, garlic, honey and seasoning to taste. Put the tomatoes into a small strainer and press the juice through, adding it to the fromage frais mixture. Cut the tomato flesh into thin strips and add to the mixture with the quail's eggs, avocado and basil, pile into the filo cases and garnish with sprigs of basil.

Freezing: is recommended for the filo flower cases. These will keep for up to 3 months. Pack them with tissue paper in a rigid, freezerproof container as they are very brittle. Remove from the container and leave at room temperature for 10 minutes before use.

SERVES 6

Nutritional content per serving: Carbohydrate: 4 Fat: 3 Kilocalories: 65

Paw-Paw and Tofu Vinaigrette

75 g (3 oz) tofu (bean curd)
1 paw-paw, peeled, halved and seeded
2 kiwi fruit, peeled
2 tablespoons pine kernels, toasted
LIME DRESSING:
6 tablespoons olive oil
3 tablespoons lime juice
1 tablespoon clear honey
2 tablespoons chopped chervil
salt and pepper

Slice the tofu thinly, then cut into strips and place in a shallow dish. Put all the dressing ingredients together in a screw-top jar and shake vigorously to mix. Pour over the tofu and leave to marinate for 1 hour.

Cut the paw-paw lengthways into slices. Slice the kiwi fruit and arrange on individual plates with the paw-paw slices and the tofu. Spoon the dressing over each plate and sprinkle with the pine kernels.

SERVES 6

Nutritional content per serving: Carbohydrate: 7 Fat: 19 Fibre: 1 Kilocalories: 215

Filo Flowers; Paw-Paw and Tofu Vinaigrette

Garlic and Cashew Nut Soup

125 g (4 oz) white bread, crusts removed
150 ml (¼ pint) milk
15 g (½ oz) fresh parsley, stalks removed
125 g (4 oz) cashew nuts
2 cloves garlic
3 tablespoons olive oil
3 tablespoons cider vinegar
450 ml (¾ pint) water
salt and pepper
chervil sprigs to garnish

Break the bread into pieces and put into a bowl, pour over the milk and leave to soak for 5 minutes. Put into a blender or food processor with the parsley, nuts, garlic, oil, vinegar and water and seasoning to taste. Blend for about 1 minute until smooth, then chill for 1 hour.

Spoon the chilled soup into individual bowls and garnish with sprigs of chervil.

Freezing: is recommended. Pour into a rigid freezerproof container, cover and freeze. The soup will keep for up to 1 month. Defrost overnight in the refrigerator or at room temperature for 4 hours and stir well to blend before serving.

SERVES 4–6

Nutritional content per serving: Carbohydrate: 27 Fat: 27 Fibre: 2 Kilocalories: 380

Potage Catalan

A THICK, HEARTY SOUP OF CHICKPEAS AND VEGETABLES – SERVED WITH CRUSTY BREAD IT'S A MEAL IN ITSELF

2 tablespoons olive oil
1 large onion, chopped
2 cloves garlic, chopped
2 carrots, chopped
1 turnip, chopped
2 celery sticks, chopped
1 × 400 g (14 oz) can chopped tomatoes
1.25 litres (2 pints) water or vegetable stock
1 bay leaf
175 g (6 oz) cabbage, shredded
1 × 425 g (15 oz) can chickpeas, drained
2 tablespoons chopped parsley
salt and pepper

Heat the oil in a large saucepan and fry the onion and garlic until softened. Add the carrots, turnip, celery, tomatoes, water or stock, bay leaf and seasoning to taste. Bring to the boil, cover and simmer gently for 40 minutes.

Add the cabbage and chickpeas and cook for a further 20 minutes. Stir in the parsley and pour into a large warmed tureen or individual soup bowls.

Microwave: Microwave the oil, onion and garlic on Full Power for 3 minutes. Add the carrots, turnip, celery and tomatoes, cover and microwave on Full Power for 15–20 minutes, stirring once, until the vegetables are almost tender. Add the stock, bay leaf and seasoning to taste. Cover and microwave on Full Power for 10 minutes. Add cabbage and chickpeas and microwave on Full Power for a further 10 minutes. Stir in the parsley and serve as above.

SERVES 6

Nutritional content per serving: Carbohydrate: 21 Fat: 7 Fibre: 8 Kilocalories: 175

Garlic and Cashew Nut Soup; Potage Catalan (bottom); Mushroom Ragoût

MUSHROOM RAGOÛT

- 1 tablespoon olive oil
- 15 g (½ oz) butter
- 1 onion, chopped
- 2 cloves garlic, chopped
- 375 g (12 oz) button mushrooms
- 1 tablespoon brandy or Madeira
- 75 ml (3 fl oz) double cream
- 1 teaspoon chopped thyme
- salt and pepper
- 1 tablespoon chopped parsley to garnish

Heat the oil and butter in a frying pan and fry the onion until softened. Add the garlic and mushrooms and fry quickly, stirring occasionally, for 3 minutes.

Add the brandy or Madeira, cream, thyme and seasoning to taste, bring to the boil and simmer for 2–3 minutes.

Turn into a heated serving dish, sprinkle with parsley and serve with crusty bread.

SERVES 4

Nutritional content per serving: Carbohydrate: 4 Fat: 16 Fibre: 4 Kilocalories: 180

Iced Tomato and Basil Soup

300 g (10 oz) natural yogurt
300 ml (½ pint) tomato juice
150 ml (¼ pint) milk
1 clove garlic, crushed
3 tomatoes, skinned and chopped finely
3 tablespoons chopped basil
salt and pepper
basil sprigs to garnish

Mix the yogurt, tomato juice and milk together in a bowl until blended. Stir in the garlic, tomatoes, basil and seasoning to taste, then chill for approximately 1 hour.

Pour into bowls and garnish with sprigs of basil.

SERVES 4

Nutritional content per serving: Carbohydrate: 9 Fat: 2 Fibre: 1 Kilocalories: 80

Stuffed Vine Leaves

PACKETS OF VINE LEAVES ARE READILY AVAILABLE NOW, BUT IF YOU ARE LUCKY ENOUGH TO HAVE A VINE GROWING IN YOUR GARDEN, CHOOSE ONLY THE UNBLEMISHED LEAVES AND BLANCH THEM IN BOILING WATER FOR 2 MINUTES

250 g (8 oz) preserved vine leaves, drained
about 75 g (3 oz) bulgar wheat
about 450 ml (¾ pint) boiling water
1 onion, chopped
2 cloves garlic
1 tablespoon tomato purée
1 teaspoon ground cumin
2 tablespoons chopped dill or mint
2 tablespoons pine kernels
25 g (1 oz) currants
2 tablespoons olive oil
300 ml (½ pint) water
4 tablespoons lemon juice
salt and pepper
lemon wedges to serve

Rinse the vine leaves well, under cold running water to rid them of excess salt. Pour the boiling water over the bulgar wheat and leave to soak for 30 minutes. Tip the wheat into a strainer lined with muslin, then squeeze the muslin to extract as much water as possible.

Mix the bulgar wheat with the onion, garlic, tomato purée, cumin, dill or mint, pine kernels, currants and seasoning to taste.

Place a spoonful of the filling on to one vine leaf with the vein side upwards. Fold the stem up over the filling, fold both sides toward the middle, then roll into a small parcel.

Line the bottom of a casserole dish with any damaged vine leaves, then pack the stuffed vine leaves on top in layers, wedged closely together, so that they do not unroll during cooking.

Mix the oil with the water and lemon juice and pour over the vine leaves. Cover and cook in a preheated oven 180°C, 350°F, Gas Mark 4 for 1 hour.

Leave to cool in the casserole and serve cold with lemon wedges.

Microwave: To defrost after freezing, microwave on Defrost for 10–15 minutes until no longer firm and frozen. Leave to stand for 5 minutes.

Freezing: is recommended. Pack closely into a rigid container, cover, seal and freeze. This will keep for up to 3 months. Defrost overnight in the refrigerator or at room temperature for 4 hours.

SERVES 8

Nutritional content per serving: Carbohydrate: 9 Fat: 6 Fibre: 3 Kilocalories: 100

Iced Tomato and Basil Soup; Stuffed Vine Leaves (bottom); Marinated Goat's Cheese

MARINATED GOAT'S CHEESE

CROTTIN DE CHAVIGNOL IS AN EXCELLENT CHEESE FOR THIS RECIPE. YOU CAN ADD MORE CHEESE TO THE OIL TO REPLACE WHAT YOU HAVE USED OR ALTERNATIVELY DRESS SALADS WITH THE DRAINED OIL

2 x 100 g (3½ oz) rolls goat's cheese
2 bay leaves
2 sprigs thyme
1 teaspoon black peppercorns
2 small dried red chillies (optional)
250 ml (8 fl oz) (approximately) olive oil
thyme sprigs to garnish

Cut each cheese into 4 slices about 8 mm (⅜ inch) thick and put into a wide-necked glass jar or plastic container, to fit snugly. Put in the bay leaves, thyme, peppercorns and chillies if using, then pour in the oil to cover the cheese.

Cover with the lid and leave for 2 weeks. The cheese will keep for up to 8 weeks, but becomes soft if left longer.

Place 2 slices of the cheese on each plate, garnish with a sprig of thyme and serve with rye bread.

SERVES 4

Nutritional content per serving: Fat: 12 Kilocalories: 150

GOAT'S CHEESE IN FILO PASTRY

2 sheets filo pastry
25 g (1 oz) butter, melted
2 × 100 g (3½ oz) rolls goat's cheese
oil for deep frying
WATERCRESS SAUCE:
1 bunch watercress
150 g (5 oz) natural yogurt
1 teaspoon lemon juice
½ teaspoon clear honey
salt and pepper

Cut the filo pastry into 12 × 15 cm (5 × 6 inch) squares. Make into a pile and cover with a cloth to prevent them drying out. Brush one pastry square with butter, lay another square on top and brush with a little more butter. Cut the goat's cheeses into 6 slices and lay 1 slice on the pastry square. Gather up the edges of the pastry and pinch together into a money-bag shape – the butter will help the pastry to stick together. Repeat with the remaining pastry and cheese to make a total of 6 parcels.

To make the sauce, blanch all but 6 sprigs of watercress in boiling water for 2 minutes and drain well. Put in a blender or food processor with the remaining ingredients and blend until smooth. Turn into a saucepan and warm gently, but be careful not to boil or it will curdle.

Heat the oil to 180°C, 350°F or until a cube of bread dropped in turns brown in 30 seconds. Place 3 parcels in a deep frying basket and fry for 2 minutes until crisp and golden, turning once. Drain thoroughly on kitchen paper, then repeat with the remaining parcels.

Put 2 tablespoonfuls of the sauce on each serving plate, place a parcel in the centre of the sauce and garnish with a sprig of the reserved watercress.

Freezing: is recommended for the parcels. Freeze before frying. Pack into a rigid freezerproof container in one layer, cover, seal and freeze. These will keep for up to 3 months. Defrost at room temperature for 3 hours.

SERVES 6

Nutritional content per serving: Carbohydrate: 7 Fat: 32 Kilocalories: 375

SESAME CREAM

75 ml (3 fl oz) tahini paste
2 cloves garlic
3 large sprigs parsley
3 tablespoons water
4 tablespoons lemon juice
75 ml (3 fl oz) natural fromage frais
salt and pepper
TO GARNISH:
black olives
quail's eggs, hard-boiled and halved
parsley sprigs

Put the tahini paste, garlic, parsley and water in a blender or food processor and blend until smooth. Add the lemon juice, fromage frais and seasoning to taste and blend again to make a smooth cream, then turn into a shallow serving dish.

Garnish with olives, quail's eggs and parsley and serve with sliced pitta bread.

SERVES 6

Nutritional content per serving: Carbohydrate: 3 Fat: 9 Fibre: 1 Kilocalories: 105

Sesame Cream; Goat's Cheese in Filo Pastry (top); Tomato and Avocado Timbales

Tomato and Avocado Timbales

450 ml (3/4 pint) tomato juice
1 clove garlic, crushed
1 teaspoon clear honey
3 tablespoons olive oil
1 tablespoon cider vinegar
2 teaspoons chopped basil
4 tablespoons cold water
15 g (1/2 oz) agar agar powder
2 avocados
2 tomatoes, skinned and chopped finely
1 tablespoon lemon juice
salt and pepper
basil sprigs to garnish

Put the tomato juice, garlic, honey, oil, vinegar and basil into a bowl with seasoning to taste and mix together thoroughly.

Put the water into a small saucepan, sprinkle over the agar agar and leave to soak for 5 minutes. Boil for 10 minutes until dissolved then add to the tomato liquid.

Cut one of the avocados into 1 cm (1/2 inch) dice and add to the tomato liquid with the chopped tomatoes. Mix well.

Pour into 6 × 150 ml (1/4 pint) ramekins and chill for approximately 2 hours until set.

Dip the ramekins in hot water for an instant to loosen, then turn the timbales on to individual serving plates and garnish with sliced avocado brushed with lemon juice and basil sprigs.

SERVES 6

Nutritional content per serving: Carbohydrate: 4 Fat: 22 Fibre: 2 Kilocalories: 230

CALDO VERDE

A NOURISHING SOUP OF POTATO AND SPRING GREENS FROM PORTUGAL

2 tablespoons olive oil
1 large onion, chopped
2 cloves garlic, chopped
500 g (1 lb) potatoes, cut into 2.5 cm (1 inch) cubes
1.25 litres (2 pints) water or vegetable stock
250 g (8 oz) spring greens, shredded finely
2 tablespoons chopped parsley
salt and pepper

Heat the oil in a pan and fry the onion for 5 minutes until softened but still clear. Add the garlic and potatoes and cook for a few minutes, stirring occasionally.

Add the water or stock with seasoning to taste and cook for 15 minutes until the potatoes are tender. Mash the potatoes roughly in their liquid, then add the greens and boil uncovered for 10 minutes. Add the parsley and simmer for 2–3 minutes until heated through.

SERVES 6

Nutritional content per serving: Carbohydrate: 28 Fat: 5 Fibre: 4 Kilocalories: 125

SOUP AU PISTOU

A DELICIOUS VEGETABLE SOUP FROM PROVENCE WITH A PASTE OF BASIL, PARMESAN AND GARLIC ADDED JUST BEFORE SERVING. YOU CAN USE A BOUGHT PREPARATION CALLED PESTO, IF YOU PREFER. THIS IS MADE WITH THE SAME INGREDIENTS BUT ALSO INCLUDES PINE KERNELS

3 tablespoons olive oil
1 onion, chopped
1 clove garlic, chopped
3 carrots, sliced thinly
3 celery sticks, sliced thinly
2 leeks, sliced thinly
1.75 litres (3 pints) water or vegetable stock
125 g (4 oz) green beans, cut into 3 cm (1½ inch) lengths
2 tablespoons tomato purée
1 bouquet garni
1 large potato, chopped roughly
3 tomatoes, skinned and chopped
1 x 432 g (15 oz) can cannellini beans, drained
salt and pepper
basil sprigs to garnish
PISTOU:
large bunch fresh basil
2 cloves garlic
25 g (1 oz) Parmesan cheese
3 tablespoons olive oil

Heat the oil in a large saucepan and gently fry the onion, garlic, carrots, celery and leeks for 10 minutes, stirring occasionally.

Add the water or stock, green beans, tomato purée, bouquet garni, potato and seasoning to taste. Cover and simmer over a low heat for 45 minutes.

Meanwhile, make the pistou. Put all the ingredients in a blender or food processor and blend until smooth. Scrape the sides of the blender or food processor down and blend again.

Add the pistou to the soup with the tomatoes and beans and heat through. Garnish with basil and serve.

The pistou can be stored in a small jar. Pour a thin layer of oil over the top to preserve it.

Freezing: is recommended. Pour into a rigid freezerproof container, cool, seal and freeze. The soup will keep for up to 2 months. Defrost at room temperature for 4 hours then reheat in a saucepan.

SERVES 8

Nutritional content per serving: Carbohydrate: 17 Fat: 12 Fibre: 5 Kilocalories: 200

Caldo Verde; Soup au Pistou

WARM BROCCOLI VINAIGRETTE

375 g (12 oz) broccoli
250 g (8 oz) cauliflower
2 tablespoons pine kernels, toasted
DRESSING:
2 tablespoons tarragon vinegar
2 tablespoons coarse grain mustard
3 tablespoons olive oil
2 tablespoons double cream
salt and pepper

Break the broccoli and cauliflower into small florets and cook in boiling salted water for 5 minutes. Drain thoroughly, put in a bowl and cover to keep warm.

To make the dressing, mix the vinegar, mustard and seasoning together, then gradually whisk in the oil until it thickens. Stir in the cream and pour the dressing over the florets, tossing carefully until well coated.

Arrange on individual plates and sprinkle with the pine kernels.

SERVES 4

Nutritional content per serving: Carbohydrate: 2 Fat: 10 Fibre: 5 Kilocalories: 210

Warm Broccoli Vinaigrette; Smoked Tofu with Seaweed (bottom); Asparagus Croustades

Asparagus croustades

- 1 large unsliced wholemeal sandwich loaf
- 3 tablespoons safflower oil
- tarragon sprigs to garnish

FILLING:

- 125 g (4 oz) asparagus
- 2 tablespoons sunflower oil
- 1 onion, sliced
- 125 g (4 oz) button mushrooms
- 2 tablespoons plain flour
- 1 tablespoon chopped tarragon
- 2 tablespoons single cream
- salt and pepper

Cut 4 × 3.5 cm (1½ inch) slices from the loaf then cut into 7.5 cm (3 inch) squares. Cut out the centre, leaving a 5 mm (¼ inch) border all the way round and a base. Brush all over with the oil, place on a baking sheet and bake in a preheated oven, 200°C, 400°F, Gas Mark 6 for 10 minutes until the squares are crisp and golden brown.

Cut the asparagus into 3.5 cm (1½ inch) lengths and set the tips aside. Cook the stalks in boiling water for 5 minutes, add the tips and cook for a further 3 minutes. Drain, reserving the liquid, and set aside.

Heat the oil in a pan and fry the onion until softened. Add the mushrooms and cook for a further 2 minutes, stirring occasionally. Remove from the heat, stir in the flour, then gradually add 250 ml (8 fl oz) of the reserved liquid and the tarragon. Bring to the boil, stirring, and cook for 2 minutes. Add the cream, asparagus and seasoning to taste.

Spoon into the warmed bread croustades, garnish with the tarragon sprigs and serve on individual plates.

Freezing: is recommended for the croustades. Freeze after baking; pack into a polythene bag, seal and freeze. These will keep for up to 3 months. To defrost, unwrap and reheat from frozen for 5–7 minutes.

SERVES 4

Nutritional content per serving: Carbohydrate: 30 Fat: 22 Fibre: 6 Kilocalories: 340

Smoked tofu with seaweed

Spring greens or cabbage are often used in Chinese restaurants for the fried seaweed you find on the menu. Very easy to do, but be sure the greens are absolutely dry before frying

- 375 g (12 oz) spring greens or cabbage, tough stalks removed
- oil for deep frying
- 1 teaspoon caster sugar
- 1 teaspoon sesame oil
- 125 g (4 oz) smoked tofu (bean curd) cut into slices
- 1 tablespoon sesame seeds, toasted
- 4 radish roses to garnish

Lay the spring greens or cabbage leaves one on top of another and form a tight roll. Shred very finely with a sharp knife.

Heat the oil to 180°C, 350°F or until a cube of bread dropped in browns in 30 seconds, then carefully add the shredded greens in batches. Fry for 10 seconds, then remove and drain well on kitchen paper. Turn into a bowl, sprinkle with the sugar and keep warm.

Heat the sesame oil in a small pan and fry the tofu for 1 minute, turning once.

Arrange a pile of 'seaweed' on each serving dish, top with the fried tofu and sprinkle with sesame seeds. Garnish with radish roses.

SERVES 4

Nutritional content per serving: Carbohydrate: 5 Fat: 10 Fibre: 3 Kilocalories: 125

OLIVE DIP WITH CRUDITÉS

2 tablespoons olive oil
1 onion, chopped
2 cloves garlic
1 tablespoon tomato purée
1 tablespoon capers
125 g (4 oz) black olives, pitted
1 X 432 g (15 oz) can red kidney beans, drained
2 tablespoons water
CRUDITÉS
1 head chicory, separated into leaves
1 bunch radishes, topped and tailed
a few heads broccoli, broken into florets
1/2 small cauliflower, broken into florets
8 quail's eggs, hard-boiled
small bunch baby carrots, topped and tailed

Heat the oil and fry the onion until softened. Add the garlic and fry for a further minute then stir in the tomato purée and capers and leave the mixture to cool.

Put the olives and beans into a blender or food processor with the water and blend until smooth. Add the fried mixture through the feeder tube or through the hole in the lid, a third at a time, adding a little more water if necessary to achieve a consistency similar to a thick mayonnaise.

Arrange the crudités decoratively on a serving plate and serve with the olive dip.

Freezing: is recommended for the dip. Turn into a rigid freezerproof container, cover, seal and freeze. This will keep for up to 1 month. Defrost overnight in the refrigerator or at room temperature for 4 hours. Stir well before serving.

SERVES 8

Nutritional content per serving: Carbohydrate: 11 Fat: 6 Fibre: 8 Kilocalories: 115

AUBERGINE AND CHEESE TIMBALES

1 large aubergine
5 tablespoons olive oil
1 onion, chopped
1 clove garlic, chopped
1 X 400 g (14 oz) can chopped tomatoes
125 g (4 oz) curd cheese
1 egg
1 tablespoon chopped basil
salt and pepper
basil sprigs to garnish

Slice the aubergine, sprinkle with salt and leave in a colander for 1 hour. Rinse well and pat dry on kitchen paper.

Heat 2 tablespoons of oil in a pan and fry the onion until softened, add the garlic and tomatoes, season to taste and simmer for 5 minutes. Pour into a sieve and leave to drain.

Mix the cheese with the egg and basil and season to taste.

Heat a further 2 tablespoons of oil in a pan and fry the aubergine until beginning to colour. Press down firmly with a fish slice to extract oil, brush the top with the remaining oil if necessary then turn and cook on the second side. Drain on kitchen paper.

Arrange an aubergine slice in the base of 4 small greased ramekins. Put a spoonful of tomato pulp on the aubergine, then a spoonful of cheese mixture, and top with an aubergine slice. Cover with foil and bake in a preheated oven, 180°C, 350°F, Gas Mark 4 for 30 minutes until set.

Meanwhile, sieve the remaining tomato pulp, pour into a saucepan and heat through. Turn the timbales on to individual serving plates, surround with the sauce and garnish with the basil sprigs.

SERVES 4

Nutritional content per serving: Carbohydrate: 4 Fat: 30 Fibre: 1 Kilocalories: 375

Olive Dip with Crudités; Aubergine and Cheese Timbales (bottom); Warm Leeks with Herbs

WARM LEEKS WITH HERBS

FRENCH DRESSING IS QUICK AND EASY, USE 5 TABLESPOONS OLIVE OIL, 2 TABLESPOONS CIDER VINEGAR, 1 TEASPOON COARSE GRAIN MUSTARD, ½ TEASPOON CLEAR HONEY, 1 CLOVE GARLIC, CRUSHED AND SALT AND PEPPER. PLACE ALL THE INGREDIENTS IN A SCREW-TOP JAR AND SHAKE VIGOROUSLY. THIS WILL KEEP IN THE JAR IN THE REFRIGERATOR FOR SEVERAL WEEKS. SHAKE WELL BEFORE USING

500 g (1 lb) thin leeks
8 tablespoons French dressing
3 tablespoons chopped herbs such as chives, parsley and thyme
4 tablespoons natural fromage frais
salt

Trim the leeks to about 15 cm (6 inches), split lengthways and wash thoroughly. Cook in boiling salted water for 8 minutes until tender, then drain thoroughly, pressing out all liquid. Arrange on a serving dish and set aside.

Add the herbs and fromage frais to the French dressing and whisk until emulsified. Pour over the leeks while still warm and serve immediately with brown bread.

SERVES 4

Nutritional content per serving: Carbohydrate: 8 Fat: 9 Fibre: 5 Kilocalories: 130

CHOUX PUFFS WITH MUSHROOMS

IF YOU HAVE ACCESS TO WILD MUSHROOMS, THESE MAKE AN EXCELLENT ALTERNATIVE TO FIELD MUSHROOMS

50 g (2 oz) margarine
150 ml (1/4 pint) water
65 g (2 1/2 oz) plain flour, sifted
1 teaspoon dried mustard powder, sifted
2 eggs
50 g (2 oz) Cheddar cheese, grated
1 tablespoon sesame seeds
thyme sprigs to garnish
MUSHROOM FILLING:
4 tablespoons olive oil
8 spring onions, chopped
4 cloves garlic, chopped
375 g (12 oz) field or chestnut mushrooms, chopped
2 rounded tablespoons plain flour
300 ml (1/2 pint) milk
2 teaspoons chopped thyme
6 tablespoons single cream
2 tablespoons dry sherry
salt and pepper

Melt the margarine in a large saucepan, add the water and bring to the boil. Remove from the heat and shoot in the flour and mustard all at once, beating vigorously with a wooden spoon until the mixture leaves the sides of the pan clean. Add the eggs one at a time until the mixture thickens again, then mix in the cheese.

Spoon 8 mounds on to greased baking sheets and sprinkle with the sesame seeds. Bake in a preheated oven, 200°C, 400°F, Gas Mark 6 for 25–30 minutes until crisp and golden brown.

For the filling, heat the oil in a pan and fry the onions and garlic for 2 minutes. Add the mushrooms and cook for 3 minutes, stirring occasionally. Remove from the heat and stir in the flour then gradually add the milk, stirring until combined. Add the thyme and seasoning to taste then bring to the boil and cook for 2 minutes until thickened.

Put a quarter of the mixture into a blender or food processor with the cream and sherry and blend until smooth. Turn this sauce into another saucepan and keep warm.

When the puffs are cooked, split them in half with a knife and fill each with a quarter of the remaining mushroom mixture. Pour the sauce on to 4 serving plates, sit a mushroom puff on each and garnish with a sprig of thyme.

Microwave: Prepare and cook the puffs as above. To make the filling, microwave the oil, onions and garlic on Full Power for 2 minutes. Add the mushrooms, cover and microwave on Full Power for 4 minutes, stirring once. Add the flour, milk, thyme and seasoning to taste. Microwave on Full Power for 4–5 minutes, stirring twice until thickened. Remove a quarter and purée with the cream and sherry. Reheat on Full Power for 1/2–1 minute. Then fill and serve the choux puffs as above.

Freezing: is recommended for the choux puffs. Place in a polythene bag, seal and freeze. These will keep for up to 3 months. Reheat from frozen in a preheated oven, 200°C, 400°F, Gas Mark 6 for 10 minutes.

SERVES 8

Nutritional content per serving: Carbohydrate: 11 Fat: 20 Fibre: 2 Kilocalories: 250

Choux Puffs with Mushrooms; Tomato Ice

TOMATO ICE

500 g (1 lb) tomatoes, chopped roughly
1 small clove garlic, chopped
½ bay leaf
4 sprigs basil
1 tablespoon tomato purée
1 tablespoon clear honey
1 tablespoon lemon juice
¼ teaspoon Tabasco sauce
150 ml (¼ pint) mayonnaise
¼ cucumber, sliced thinly
salt and pepper
TO GARNISH:
4 tomato roses
basil sprigs

Put the tomatoes in a pan with the garlic, herbs, tomato purée, honey, lemon juice and Tabasco sauce with seasoning to taste. Bring to the boil, simmer gently for 5 minutes, then sieve and allow to cool.

Freeze the mixture for 4 hours until half frozen then put into a blender or food processor and blend until smooth. Add the mayonnaise and blend again until incorporated. Turn into a rigid, freezerproof container and freeze until solid.

Remove from the freezer and place in the refrigerator for 30 minutes then use two dessertspoons dipped in cold water to form 12 oval shapes from the tomato ice. Place on foil and freeze to harden.

To make a tomato rose, take a firm tomato and, with a sharp knife, peel off the skin in a continuous strip about 1 cm (½ inch) wide, starting at the base. With the fleshy side inside, start to curl from the base end to form a bud shape then wind the strip of skin into a rose.

Arrange the cucumber in overlapping circles around 4 individual serving plates. Place 3 ovals of tomato ice on each plate, garnish with a tomato rose and basil sprigs and serve immediately.

SERVES 4

Nutritional content per serving: Carbohydrate: 8 Fat: 30 Fibre: 2 Kilocalories: 305

CHEESE AND EGG DISHES

THERE ARE NOW MANY VEGETARIAN CHEESES AVAILABLE MADE WITH VEGETABLE RENNET, GIVING A MUCH WIDER CHOICE TO STRICT VEGETARIANS. EGGS ARE READILY AVAILABLE, EASY TO PREPARE AND DIGEST, AND ALSO INEXPENSIVE. USE FREE RANGE WHEN POSSIBLE AS THEY HAVE A SUPERIOR FLAVOUR.

CALZONE

CALZONE IS A TYPE OF CLOSED PIZZA MADE WITH BREAD DOUGH, WHICH HAS FILLINGS AS VARIED AS PIZZA TOPPINGS. WHILE PIZZA IS ALMOST ALWAYS ROUND, THE SHAPE OF CALZONE CAN DIFFER FROM ONE REGION OF ITALY TO ANOTHER. CRESCENTS, SQUARES AND TRIANGLES ARE ALL TO BE FOUND

500 g (1 lb) plain flour, sifted
1 teaspoon salt
15 g (½ oz) fresh yeast
300 ml (½ pint) warm water
marjoram sprigs to garnish
FILLING:
2 tablespoons olive oil
2 large onions, sliced
4 tomatoes, skinned and chopped
1 tablespoon tomato purée
125 g (4 oz) black olives, pitted and chopped
1 tablespoon capers
1 teaspoon chopped oregano
250 g (8 oz) Mozzarella cheese, cubed
milk for brushing
1 tablespoon sesame seeds
salt and pepper

Place the flour and salt in a mixing bowl and make a well in the centre.

Cream the yeast with a little of the water and leave until frothy. Add to the flour with the remaining water and mix to a soft dough. Turn on to a floured surface and knead for about 5 minutes until smooth and elastic. Return to the bowl, cover with a damp tea towel and leave to rise in a warm place until doubled in size.

To make the filling, heat the oil in a pan and fry the onions until softened. Add the tomatoes and tomato purée, olives and capers, and cook for about 5 minutes. Stir in the oregano with seasoning to taste, then leave to cool.

Turn the dough on to a floured surface, knead for a few minutes, then divide into 6 pieces. Roll out each piece into a 23 cm (9 inch) circle. Spread some filling over one half of each circle, leaving a small border, and sprinkle with Mozzarella cheese. Moisten the edge, fold over and press the edges together to seal. Brush with milk, sprinkle with sesame seeds and leave to rise in a warm place for 15 minutes.

Bake in a preheated oven, 220°C, 425°F, Gas Mark 7 for 10–15 minutes until puffed up and golden.

Garnish with marjoram sprigs and serve.

MAKES 6

Nutritional content per serving: Carbohydrate: 73 Fat: 19 Fibre: 6 Kilocalories: 525

MENEMEN

A POPULAR EGG DISH IN TURKEY, OFTEN SERVED AT BREAKFAST WITH FRESH BREAD, WARM FROM THE BRICK OVEN

2 tablespoons olive oil
1 onion, chopped
2 large red peppers, cored, deseeded and chopped
4 tomatoes, peeled and chopped
8 eggs
salt and pepper
TO GARNISH:
chervil sprigs
2 tablespoons chopped parsley

Heat the oil in a frying pan and fry the onion and peppers for 10 minutes, stirring occasionally. Add the tomatoes with seasoning to taste and cook for a further 5 minutes.

Beat the eggs together in a bowl then add to the vegetables. Stir occasionally until set. Garnish with chervil sprigs and serve on individual plates sprinkled with parsley.

SERVES 4

Nutritional content per serving: Carbohydrate: 12 Fat: 12 Fibre: 3 Kilocalories: 245

Calzone; Menemen

CHEESE AND ONION PIE

2 tablespoons olive oil
2 onions, chopped
2 eggs
125 ml (4 fl oz) milk
250 g (8 oz) Cheddar cheese, grated
1 teaspoon dried mustard powder
50 g (2 oz) butter, melted
10–12 sheets filo pastry
1 teaspoon sesame seeds
salt and pepper

Heat the oil in a pan and fry the onions until softened. Mix the eggs and milk together then stir in the onions, cheese, mustard powder and seasoning to taste.

Butter a 18 × 28 cm (7 inch × 11 inch) baking tin and line with a sheet of filo pastry, leaving the edges overlapping. Brush with melted butter and lay another sheet over it, brush again with butter and continue until you have 5 or 6 layers of pastry. Cover the remaining sheets of filo pastry with a damp cloth so that they do not dry out and become brittle and difficult to handle.

Pour the filling into the lined tin. Cover with the remaining filo sheets, brushing each with melted butter, and trim the edges closely to fit the tin. Fold the bottom edges over the top to make a lip and brush with butter so that they seal well. Brush the top with the remaining butter, sprinkle with sesame seeds and leave for 5 minutes for the butter to set, then cut through the top of the pie, marking it into 6. Bake in a preheated oven, 190°C, 375°F, Gas Mark 5 for 35–40 minutes until crisp and golden. Serve with a salad.

Freezing: is recommended. Before baking, cover with foil, seal the edges and freeze. This will keep for up to 3 months. Cook from frozen, removing the foil first, for 40–45 minutes.

SERVES 6

Nutritional content per serving: Carbohydrate: 15 Fat: 29 Fibre: 1 Kilocalories: 380

BAKED EGG WITH POTATO AND ONION

500 g (1 lb) potatoes
2 tablespoons olive oil
1 large onion, sliced
1 clove garlic, chopped
2 tablespoons vegetable stock
1 tablespoon chopped parsley
2 eggs
50 g (2 oz) Gruyère or Cheddar cheese
salt and pepper

Cut the potatoes into strips measuring 3 mm × 2.5 cm (1/8 × 1 inch).

Heat the oil in a heavy-based pan and fry the onion for 5 minutes. Add the garlic and potatoes and fry for 15 minutes, stirring occasionally. Add the stock, cover and cook for a further 5 minutes, then stir in the parsley with seasoning to taste.

Turn into 2 greased ovenproof dishes and make a well in the centre of each. Crack an egg into each well and sprinkle with cheese.

Bake in a preheated oven, 190°C, 375°F, Gas Mark 5 for 10 minutes until the egg white has set.

SERVES 2

Nutritional content per serving: Carbohydrate: 55 Fat: 29 Fibre: 4 Kilocalories: 530

Cheese and Onion Pie; Omelette Roulade (top); Baked Egg with Potato and Onion

Omelette Roulade

15 g (½ oz) dried cep mushrooms or
  25 g (1 oz) chestnut mushrooms
2 tablespoons olive oil
1 onion, chopped
1 clove garlic
125 g (4 oz) mushrooms, sliced
2 tablespoons chopped dill
4 tablespoons natural fromage frais
a few lettuce leaves
3 eggs
salt and pepper
chervil sprigs to garnish

Pour boiling water over the dried mushrooms to cover and leave to soak for 30 minutes then drain. Chop the mushrooms.

Heat the oil in a pan and fry the onion until softened. Add the garlic, both types of mushrooms and cook, stirring occasionally, for a further 3–4 minutes. Allow to cool, then mix in the dill and fromage frais with seasoning to taste. Blanch the lettuce leaves in boiling salted water for 1 minute to soften.

Beat the eggs together with seasoning to taste. Heat a 23 cm (9 inch) omelette pan and oil lightly. Pour in half the egg mixture, tilting the pan to coat the bottom evenly, and cook until the omelette is set. Remove from the pan and make a second omelette in the same way. Lay the omelettes on a work surface, overlapping them slightly to make a figure 8. Lay lettuce leaves over the top.

Cover with the mushroom filling and, starting at one narrow end, roll up like a Swiss roll. Cut into slices with a sharp knife. Garnish with chervil sprigs and serve hot.

SERVES 2

Nutritional content per serving: Carbohydrate: 6 Fat: 26 Fibre: 2 Kilocalories: 310

Courgette and Mushroom Gougère

CHOUX PASTRY:
150 ml (¼ pint) water
50 g (2 oz) margarine
65 g (2½ oz) plain flour, sifted
1 teaspoon dried mustard powder, sifted
2 eggs
50 g (2 oz) mature Cheddar cheese, grated
1 tablespoon sesame seeds
FILLING:
2 tablespoons oil
1 onion, chopped
4 courgettes, sliced thinly
2 cloves garlic, chopped
125 g (4 oz) mushrooms, quartered
1 tablespoon plain flour
125 ml (4 fl oz) vegetable stock
1 tablespoon chopped chervil or parsley
salt and pepper
2 teaspoons grated Parmesan cheese

To make the pastry, heat the water in a large saucepan, add the margarine and bring to the boil. Add the flour all at once with the mustard and beat vigorously until the mixture leaves the sides of the pan clean.

Add the eggs, one at a time, beating vigorously, but carefully at first so that the mixture does not fly out of the pan. Beat in the cheese then place in spoonfuls around the edge of a greased 24 cm (9½ inch) ceramic flan dish. Sprinkle with sesame seeds.

To make the filling, heat the oil in a pan and gently fry the onion and courgettes for 10 minutes, stirring occasionally. Add the garlic and mushrooms and fry for a further 3 minutes. Stir in the flour, gradually add the stock and bring to the boil, stirring. Cook for 2 minutes until thickened, then add the chervil or parsley and seasoning to taste.

Spoon the filling into the centre of the choux ring, sprinkle over the grated cheese and bake in a preheated oven 200°C, 400°F, Gas Mark 6 for 40–45 minutes until crisp and golden.

Serve with a tossed green salad.

SERVES 4

Nutritional content per serving: Carbohydrate: 19 Fat: 27 Fibre: 3 Kilocalories: 355

Blue Cheese Fondue

1 clove garlic, halved
1 tablespoon cornflour
150 ml (¼ pint) white wine
250 g (8 oz) Stilton or Danish blue cheese, crumbled
300 ml (½ pint) soured cream
1 tablespoon chopped parsley
2 tablespoons chopped chives
salt and pepper
250 g (8 oz) baby new potatoes, boiled
125 g (4 oz) broccoli florets
125 g (4 oz) cauliflower florets

Rub the garlic clove round the inside of an earthenware fondue dish, then discard.

Blend the cornflour with a little of the wine, add the remaining wine to the fondue dish, and bring to the boil. Add the cornflour mixture and cook, stirring constantly, until thickened.

Add the cheese and stir until melted, then add the soured cream, parsley, chives and seasoning to taste.

Serve with new potatoes and broccoli and cauliflower florets to dip into the fondue.

SERVES 4–6

Nutritional content per serving: Carbohydrate: 19 Fat: 41 Fibre: 4 Kilocalories: 540

Courgette and Mushroom Gougère; Blue Cheese Fondue

Chicory au Gratin; Tomato and Cheese Roulade (top); Jerusalem Artichoke Soufflés

CHICORY AU GRATIN

IF YOU WANT TO PREPARE THIS DISH AHEAD OF TIME, BAKE IN A PREHEATED OVEN, 190°C, 370°F, GAS MARK 5 FOR 20–25 MINUTES. VEGETARIAN CHEDDAR MAY BE USED INSTEAD OF GRUYÈRE IF YOU PREFER

8 heads chicory
40 g (1½ oz) margarine
40 g (1½ oz) plain flour
75 g (3 oz) Gruyère cheese
150 ml (¼ pint) single cream
pinch of ground nutmeg
salt and pepper

Cook the chicory for 5 minutes in boiling salted water. Drain, reserving the liquid, then arrange in an ovenproof dish and keep warm.

Heat the margarine in a saucepan, remove from the heat and stir in the flour. Blend in 300 ml (½ pint) of the reserved liquid, return to the heat and boil for 3 minutes until smooth. Stir in three-quarters of the cheese, the cream, the nutmeg and seasoning to taste and pour over the chicory.

Sprinkle with the remaining cheese and place under a preheated grill until heated through and golden brown on top.

SERVES 4

Nutritional content per serving: Carbohydrate: 10 Fat: 22 Kilocalories: 270

TOMATO AND CHEESE ROULADE

50 g (2 oz) fresh wholemeal breadcrumbs
75 g (3 oz) mature Cheddar cheese, grated
125 g (4 oz) natural fromage frais
4 eggs, separated
½ teaspoon dried mustard powder
2 tablespoons dried breadcrumbs
salt and pepper
FILLING:
125 g (4 oz) natural fromage frais
3 tomatoes, skinned, deseeded and chopped
4 spring onions, chopped
2 tablespoons chopped basil
salt and pepper

Grease and line a 20 × 30 cm (8 × 12 inch) Swiss roll tin. Place the fresh breadcrumbs, Cheddar cheese, fromage frais, egg yolks, mustard and salt and pepper in a bowl and mix together. Whisk the egg whites until fairly stiff, then carefully fold into the cheese mixture with a metal spoon.

Turn the mixture into the prepared tin and bake in a preheated oven 200°C, 400°F, Gas Mark 6 for 15 minutes until risen and firm. Remove from the oven and lay a dampened tea towel over the top until cold.

To make the filling, put all the ingredients together in a bowl and mix well.

Sprinkle the dried breadcrumbs over a sheet of greaseproof paper. Turn the roulade out on to the paper and carefully peel off the lining paper. Spread evenly with the filling and roll up from a short side like a Swiss roll. Transfer to a serving dish, cut into slices using a very sharp knife and serve with a green salad.

SERVES 4

Nutritional content per serving: Carbohydrate: 12 Fat: 17 Fibre: 3 Kilocalories: 280

JERUSALEM ARTICHOKE SOUFFLÉS

IF YOU PREFER TO MAKE ONE LARGE SOUFFLÉ, TIE A DOUBLE BAND OF FOIL AROUND A GREASED 1.25 LITRE (2 PINT) SOUFFLÉ DISH TO COME 5 CM (2 INCHES) ABOVE THE RIM AND COOK FOR 25–30 MINUTES

2 tablespoons dried breadcrumbs
250 g (8 oz) Jerusalem artichokes
25 g (1 oz) butter or margarine
25 g (1 oz) wholemeal plain flour
150 ml (¼ pint) milk
3 eggs, separated
2 tablespoons chives
2 tablespoons parsley
salt and pepper

Grease 6 large ramekin dishes and sprinkle the breadcrumbs over the inside of each one.

Peel the artichokes, cut into chunks and cook in boiling salted water for 15 minutes until soft. Drain well, put in a blender or food processor and blend to a purée.

Melt the butter or margarine in a saucepan and stir in the flour. Remove from the heat and gradually add the milk and slowly bring to the boil, stirring. Cook for 3 minutes then add the egg yolks, artichokes, herbs and seasoning to taste and mix thoroughly.

Whisk the egg whites until fairly stiff then carefully fold into the artichoke mixture using a metal spoon.

Turn into the prepared ramekins and cook in a preheated oven, 190°C, 375°F, Gas Mark 5 for 20–25 minutes until risen and golden. Serve immediately.

SERVES 6

Nutritional content per serving: Carbohydrate: 9 Fat: 7 Fibre: 1 Kilocalories: 125

Crêpes soufflé aux épinards

BATTER:
125 g (4 oz) wholemeal plain flour
300 ml (½ pint) milk
1 egg
1 tablespoon sunflower oil
salt and pepper
FILLING:
2 tablespoons sunflower oil
3 tablespoons wholemeal plain flour
150 ml (¼ pint) milk
2 tablespoons Parmesan cheese
2 eggs, separated
250 g (8 oz) frozen chopped spinach, defrosted
¼ teaspoon grated nutmeg
TO FINISH:
15 g (½ oz) butter, melted
1 tablespoon Parmesan cheese
salad burnet or marjoram sprigs to garnish (optional)

Put the flour, milk, egg and seasoning into a blender or food processor and blend until smooth. Pour the batter into a jug and leave to stand for 30 minutes.

Heat a 15 cm (6 inch) omelette pan and add a teaspoon of oil. Pour in 1 tablespoon of the batter and tilt the pan to coat the bottom evenly. Cook until the underside is brown, then flip over and cook for 10 seconds. Turn on to a plate.

Repeat with the remaining batter, turning each crêpe out on to the plate and separating with greaseproof paper, to make 12 crêpes.

To make the filling, heat the oil in a pan and stir in the flour. Pour in the milk and stir until blended, then bring to the boil and cook for 3 minutes until thickened. Stir in the cheese, egg yolks, spinach, nutmeg and seasoning to taste. Whisk the egg whites fairly stiffly, then carefully fold into the spinach mixture.

Put a tablespoonful of the mixture on one half of each pancake and fold over the other half to enclose the filling.

Place on a greased baking sheet, brush with butter and sprinkle with Parmesan cheese. Bake in a preheated oven 200°C, 400°F, Gas Mark 6 for 15 minutes until risen and firm.

Garnish with salad burnet or marjoram sprigs, if using, and serve immediately with fresh tomato coulis (see page 54).

Microwave: Prepare and cook the crêpes as above. To make the filling, microwave the oil on Full Power for 1 minute. Stir in the flour and gradually add the milk. Microwave on Full Power for 3 minutes, stirring twice until thickened. Stir in the cheese, egg yolks, spinach, nutmeg and seasoning to taste. Whisk the egg whites and fold into the spinach mixture. Use to fill the crêpes and bake as above.

To defrost conventionally made crêpes after freezing, microwave on a plate on Medium Power for 2–2½ minutes, turning over and giving the plate a half-turn after 1½ minutes. Leave to stand for 5 minutes then peel apart to use.

Freezing: is recommended for the crêpes. Place in a polythene bag, seal and freeze. These will keep for up to 3 months. Defrost at room temperature for 1 hour.

SERVES 6

Nutritional content per serving: Carbohydrate: 23 Fat: 18 Fibre: 5 Kilocalories: 305

Crêpes Soufflé aux Épinards; Fettuccine with Walnut Sauce

Fettuccine with Walnut Sauce

250 g (8 oz) fettuccine verde
1 tablespoon olive oil
50 g (2 oz) walnuts
good bunch of chervil, stalks removed
175 g (6 oz) fromage frais
25 g (1 oz) Parmesan cheese
chervil sprigs to garnish

Cook the pasta in boiling salted water for 3–4 minutes if fresh, or 10–12 minutes if dried, or according to the instructions on the packet. Drain thoroughly, rinse well, drain again, toss in oil, then transfer to a warmed serving dish and keep warm.

Put the walnuts and chervil into a blender or food processor, and chop finely.

To make the sauce, put the fromage frais into a heavy-based pan and heat very gently, being careful not to boil. Stir in the Parmesan cheese, walnut and chervil purée and heat through gently. Pour over the pasta and garnish with sprigs of chervil.

SERVES 4

Nutritional content per serving: Carbohydrate: 53 Fat: 24 Fibre: 3 Kilocalories: 480

VEGETABLE DISHES

THERE IS SUCH AN ENORMOUS RANGE OF VEGETABLES AVAILABLE TODAY — ROOTS, STEMS, FLOWERS, LEAVES, ALL FULL OF FLAVOUR AND NUTRITIONAL VALUE IN THE FORM OF VITAMINS AND DIETARY FIBRE. THEY CAN FORM THE CENTREPIECE OF A MEAL AS WELL AS SIDE DISHES.

Potato Baskets with Broccoli

500 g (1 lb) potatoes
knob of butter
1 small egg (size 4), beaten
pinch of ground nutmeg
salt and pepper
FILLING:
175 g (6 oz) broccoli
1 tablespoon milk powder
15 g (½ oz) butter or margarine
15 g (½ oz) plain flour
25 g (1 oz) Stilton cheese, crumbled

Cook the potatoes in boiling salted water for about 20 minutes until soft. Drain well and return to the pan for a few seconds over a gentle heat to dry off. Mash the potatoes well, then add the butter, all but 1 tablespoon of the egg and seasoning to taste.

Spoon into a large piping bag fitted with a large star nozzle and pipe 4 baskets 11 cm (4½ inches) in diameter on to a greased baking sheet. Bake in a preheated oven, 220°C, 425°F, Gas Mark 7 for 15 minutes, then carefully brush with the remaining beaten egg and return to the oven for 5 minutes until crisp and golden.

Meanwhile, break the broccoli into florets and blanch in boiling water for 4 minutes. Drain, reserving 125 ml (4 fl oz) of the water, and stir in the milk powder.

Heat the butter or margarine in the same pan. Stir in the flour, then gradually add the liquid off the heat, stirring constantly until smooth. Bring to the boil and cook for 2 minutes, then stir in the Stilton. Add the broccoli and stir gently until coated with the sauce.

Put the potato baskets on serving plates and fill the centres with the broccoli mixture.

SERVES 2

Nutritional content per serving: Carbohydrate: 55 Fat: 10 Fibre: 4 Kilocalories: 340

Potato Niçoise

3 tablespoons olive oil
2 onions, chopped
2 cloves garlic, chopped
1 red pepper, cored, deseeded and chopped
1 green pepper, cored, deseeded and chopped
1 × 400 g (14 oz) can chopped tomatoes
1 tablespoon tomato purée
500 g (1 lb) potatoes, chopped roughly
1 tablespoon chopped oregano
12 black olives, halved and pitted
salt and pepper

Heat the oil in a heavy-based pan and fry the onion until softened. Add the garlic and peppers and fry for a further 5 minutes until softened, stirring occasionally.

Add the tomatoes, tomato purée, potatoes, oregano and seasoning to taste, then cover and cook for 40–45 minutes, stirring occasionally, until the potatoes are tender.

Stir in the olives and serve either warm with crusty bread or cold with a salad.

Microwave: Prepare onion mixture as above. Add remaining ingredients. Cover and microwave on Full Power for 20 minutes, stirring 3 times.

SERVES 4

Nutritional content per serving: Carbohydrate: 35 Fat: 13 Fibre: 5 Kilocalories: 270

Potato Niçoise; Potato Baskets with Broccoli

Aubergine and Potato Pie

2 large aubergines, sliced
salt
125 ml (4 fl oz) olive oil
1 onion, chopped
1 clove garlic, chopped
1 x 400 g (14 oz) can chopped tomatoes
500 g (1 lb) potatoes, boiled and sliced
125 g (4 oz) natural yogurt
1 teaspoon cornflour
1 egg
25 g (1 oz) Cheddar cheese, grated
salt and pepper

Sprinkle the aubergine slices with salt and leave in a colander for 1 hour. Rinse well and pat dry on kitchen paper.

Heat 2 tablespoons of the oil in a pan and fry the onion until softened, add the garlic and tomatoes with seasoning to taste and simmer for 5 minutes.

Heat 2 tablespoons of the remaining oil in a frying pan and fry the aubergines in 2 batches. When they begin to colour on one side press down gently with a fish slice to extract the oil, brush the tops with some remaining oil if necessary, then turn and cook on the second side. Drain on kitchen paper.

Layer the aubergines, tomato sauce and potatoes in a 1.5 litre (2½ pint) ovenproof dish, finishing with a second layer of aubergines.

Mix the yogurt and cornflour together, then mix in the egg, cheese and seasoning. Spoon over the aubergines and bake in a preheated oven, 200°C, 400°F, Gas Mark 6 for 25–30 minutes until golden.

SERVES 4

Nutritional content per serving: Carbohydrate: 34 Fat: 35 Fibre: 6 Kilocalories: 470

Feuilleté aux Champignons

2 tablespoons sunflower oil
1 onion, chopped
1 clove garlic, chopped
250 g (8 oz) mushrooms, sliced
15 g (½ oz) plain flour
125 ml (4 fl oz) milk
1 egg
1 tablespoon chopped parsley
1 teaspoon chopped thyme
salt and pepper
400 g (13 oz) puff pastry
a little milk for brushing
25 g (1 oz) Gruyère cheese, grated

Heat the oil in a pan and fry the onion until softened. Add the garlic and mushrooms and cook for a further 3 minutes. Remove from the heat and stir in the flour. Gradually add the milk, stirring continuously, then cook for 2 minutes until thickened.

Remove from the heat and stir in the egg, herbs and seasoning. Cover and leave to cool.

Divide the pastry into 4 pieces and roll each into a 17 cm (6½ inch) square and trim the edges. Put a spoonful of filling on to the centre of each square and fold over the corners to resemble an envelope. Brush the tops with a little milk and sprinkle with the cheese, then chill for 20 minutes.

Bake in a preheated oven, 200°C, 400°F, Gas Mark 6 for 25–30 minutes until well risen and golden brown. Serve with a green salad.

SERVES 4

Nutritional content per serving: Carbohydrate: 43 Fat: 43 Fibre: 4 Kilocalories: 595

Aubergine and Potato Pie; Feuilleté aux Champignons (bottom); Tagliatelle with Wild Mushrooms

TAGLIATELLE WITH WILD MUSHROOMS

50 g (2 oz) dried cep mushrooms, soaked in boiling water for 30 minutes or 125 g (4 oz) chestnut mushrooms, chopped
1 tablespoon olive oil
25 g (1 oz) butter
1 onion, chopped
1 clove garlic, chopped
125 g (4 oz) shitake or oyster mushrooms, sliced
125 g (4 oz) button mushrooms, sliced
1 tablespoon plain flour
150 ml (¼ pint) double cream
1 tablespoon chopped chervil
375–425 g (12–14 oz) fresh tagliatelle
salt and pepper
parsley or chervil sprigs to garnish

Drain the soaked mushrooms, reserving the liquid, and chop them. Heat the oil and butter in a pan and fry the onion until softened. Add the garlic, the dried and fresh mushrooms and cook, stirring occasionally, for 3 minutes. Stir in the flour then add 125 ml (4 fl oz) of the reserved mushroom liquid or water and stir continuously until thickened. Stir in the cream and chervil, with seasoning to taste, cover and simmer gently for 3 minutes.

Meanwhile, cook the tagliatelle in a large pan of boiling, salted water, according to the packet instructions, 3–4 minutes. Drain thoroughly and put into a heated serving dish, pour over the mushroom sauce and garnish with parsley or chervil sprigs.

SERVES 4

Nutritional content per serving: Carbohydrate: 39 Fat: 28 Fibre: 3 Kilocalories: 430

LEEK FLAN (TOURTE DE POIREAUX)

IF YOU PREFER YOU CAN TOP THE PIE WITH THE REMAINING PASTRY ROLLED INTO A CIRCLE INSTEAD OF THE LATTICEWORK

50 g (2 oz) butter
1 kg (2 lb) leeks, sliced
2 eggs
75 ml (3 fl oz) double cream
salt and pepper
WHOLEMEAL SHORTCRUST PASTRY:
175 g (6 oz) wholemeal plain flour
175 g (6 oz) plain flour
175 g (6 oz) margarine
3–4 tablespoons iced water
beaten egg to glaze

Melt the butter in a heavy-based saucepan and add the leeks. Cover and cook slowly, stirring occasionally, for about 20 minutes until softened. Cool slightly then gradually beat in the eggs, cream and seasoning to taste.

To make the pastry, put the flours in a mixing bowl and rub in the margarine until the mixture resembles breadcrumbs. Add enough water to mix to a firm dough, then turn on to a floured surface and knead lightly until smooth. Cut off two-thirds of the pastry, roll out thinly and use to line a 23 cm (9 inch) flan tin, leaving it overlapping at the sides.

Spread the filling evenly in the pastry case and moisten the edge of the pastry. Roll out the remaining pastry and cut into 5 mm (1/4 inch) strips. Arrange the strips in a lattice design over the filling and press the edges to secure, trimming off any excess pastry. Brush with beaten egg and bake in a preheated oven, 200°C, 400°F, Gas Mark 6 for 50–55 minutes until golden brown.

Serve warm or cold with a green salad.

Microwave: Place the butter in a bowl and microwave on Full Power for 1 1/2 minutes to melt. Add the leeks, cover and microwave on Full Power for 14 minutes, until softened, stirring twice. Add the eggs, cream and seasoning to taste. Prepare the pastry, fill the flan and bake as above.

The flan may be reheated in the microwave. Place on a double thickness piece of kitchen paper and microwave on Full Power for 2–3 minutes. Leave to stand for 2 minutes before serving.

Freezing: is recommended. Open freeze before cooking then wrap in a polythene bag, seal and return to the freezer. This will keep for up to 3 months. Cook from frozen for about 1 hour.

SERVES 6

Nutritional content per serving: Carbohydrate: 53 Fat: 39 Fibre: 9 Kilocalories: 600

Leek Flan; Broccoli and Mushroom Croustades

Broccoli and Mushroom Croustades

1 large, unsliced wholemeal sandwich loaf
3 tablespoons sunflower oil
FILLING:
250 g (8 oz) broccoli, divided into florets
2 tablespoons sunflower oil
1 onion, chopped
1 clove garlic, chopped
125 g (4 oz) button mushrooms, sliced
125 g (4 oz) full-fat soft cheese
1–2 tablespoons milk
1 tablespoon chopped chervil
1 tablespoon chopped chives
salt and pepper
chervil sprigs to garnish

Cut 4 × 3.5 cm (1 ½ inch) slices from the loaf, then cut into 10 cm (4 inch) squares. Cut out the centres, leaving a 5 mm (¼ inch) border all the way round and a base. Brush all over with the oil, place on a baking sheet and bake in a preheated oven, 200°C, 400°F, Gas Mark 6 for 10 minutes until crisp and golden brown.

To make the filling, blanch the broccoli in boiling salted water for 3 minutes, then drain. Heat the oil in a pan and fry the onion until softened. Add the garlic and mushrooms and cook for 3 minutes, stirring occasionally. Add the full-fat soft cheese and a little milk if necessary, chervil and chives and stir until blended. Stir in the broccoli, with seasoning to taste, and heat through for 5 minutes.

Spoon the mixture into the warm croustades, garnish with the chervil sprigs and serve immediately.

Freezing: is recommended for the croustades. After baking, pack into a polythene bag, seal and freeze. These will keep for up to 3 months. To defrost, unwrap and reheat from frozen for 5–7 minutes.

SERVES 4

Nutritional content per serving: Carbohydrate: 29 Fat: 29 Fibre: 9 Kilocalories: 410

TIAN D'ÉPINARDS

A TIAN IS A PEASANT DISH FROM PROVENCE WHICH TAKES ITS NAME FROM THE EARTHENWARE DISH IN WHICH IT IS TRADITIONALLY COOKED

1 kg (2 lb) spinach
3 tablespoons olive oil
1 onion, chopped
2 cloves garlic, chopped
50 g (2 oz) cooked brown rice
3 eggs
2 tablespoons chopped parsley
1/2 teaspoon grated nutmeg
1 tablespoon grated Parmesan cheese
1 tablespoon wholemeal breadcrumbs
salt and pepper

Cook the spinach in a little water for 8 minutes, drain well and chop.

Heat the oil in a frying pan, add the onion and garlic and cook until softened. Mix with the spinach, cooked rice, eggs, parsley, nutmeg and seasoning to taste, until well blended.

Turn into a greased 1.25 litre (2 pint) earthenware gratin dish and sprinkle with the cheese and breadcrumbs.

Bake in a preheated oven, 180°C, 350°F, Gas Mark 4 for 40–45 minutes.

Microwave: Microwave the spinach without any extra water on Full Power for 4–6 minutes. Drain well and chop. Continue as above.

SERVES 4

Nutritional content per serving: Carbohydrate: 20 Fat: 17 Fibre: 2 Kilocalories: 290

COURGETTE AND BEAN PROVENÇALE

175 g (6 oz) flageolet beans, soaked overnight
3 tablespoons olive oil
2 onions, sliced
2 cloves garlic, chopped
500 g (1 lb) courgettes, sliced
1 X 400 g (14 oz) can chopped tomatoes
2 tablespoons tomato purée
2 teaspoons chopped oregano
1 bouquet garni
50 g (2 oz) black olives, halved and pitted
salt and pepper
GARLIC BREAD:
1 plain or wholemeal French stick
50 g (2 oz) butter
1 clove garlic, crushed
1 tablespoon chopped parsley

Drain the beans, cover with fresh water and bring to the boil. Cover and simmer for 45 minutes to 1 hour until almost tender, adding salt towards the end of the cooking time. Drain, reserving 150 ml (1/4 pint) liquid.

Heat the oil in the pan and fry the onions until softened. Add the garlic and courgettes and fry gently, stirring occasionally, for a further 15 minutes.

Add the tomatoes, tomato purée, oregano, bouquet garni, seasoning, drained beans and reserved liquid. Cover and simmer gently for 20 minutes, adding the olives 5 minutes before the end of the cooking time.

To make the garlic bread, slice the stick diagonally three-quarters of the way through. Mix the butter, garlic, parsley and seasoning together and spread generously in each slit. Wrap in foil and bake in a preheated oven, 200°C, 400°F, Gas Mark 6 for 15 minutes. Loosen the foil and cook for a further 5 minutes to crisp.

Freezing: is recommended. Pour into a rigid freezerproof container, cover, seal and freeze. This will keep for up to 3 months. Defrost overnight in the refrigerator or at room temperature for 4 hours.

SERVES 4

Nutritional content per serving: Carbohydrate: 57 Fat: 24 Fibre: 16 Kilocalories: 500

Tian d'Épinards; Courgette and Bean Provençale (bottom); Tomato and Aubergine Crumble

Tomato and Aubergine Crumble

500 g (1 lb) aubergines, cubed
2 tablespoons olive oil
2 onions, sliced
2 cloves garlic, crushed
1 x 400 g (14 oz) can chopped tomatoes
2 teaspoons chopped oregano
1 tablespoon tomato purée
salt and pepper
parsley sprigs to garnish
HERB CRUMBLE:
150 g (5 oz) wholemeal plain flour
1 teaspoon dried mustard powder
25 g (1 oz) margarine
50 g (2 oz) Cheddar cheese, grated
3 tablespoons chopped mixed herbs

Put the aubergines in a large colander, sprinkle with salt and leave to drain for 30 minutes. Rinse well and pat dry with kitchen paper. Heat the oil in a pan, add the onions and aubergines and fry for 10 minutes, stirring occasionally. Add the garlic, tomatoes, oregano, tomato purée and seasoning. Cover and simmer for 10 minutes, then turn into a 1.5 litre (2½ pint) ovenproof dish.

To make the crumble, put the flour into a mixing bowl, sieve in the mustard and rub in the margarine until the mixture resembles breadcrumbs. Stir in the cheese and herbs.

Sprinkle over the aubergine mixture and bake in a preheated oven, 200°C, 400°F, Gas Mark 6 for 30 minutes until golden brown. Garnish with parsley sprigs and serve.

SERVES 4

Nutritional content per serving: Carbohydrate: 37 Fat: 18 Fibre: 9 Kilocalories: 340

LEEK AND POTATO GRATIN

THIS MAKES A GOOD SUPPER DISH; SERVE WITH A LEAFY SALAD

- 50 g (2 oz) butter
- 375 g (12 oz) leeks, sliced thinly
- 750 g (1½ lb) potatoes, sliced thinly
- 2 cloves garlic, chopped
- 100 g (3½ oz) roll goat's cheese
- 300 ml (½ pint) single cream
- salt and pepper

Use a quarter of the butter to grease a large, shallow ovenproof dish. Heat 25 g (1 oz) of the butter in a pan and fry the leeks gently for about 10 minutes, stirring occasionally until softened.

Arrange half the potatoes in the greased dish. Sprinkle with the garlic, leeks and seasoning to taste. Slice the goat's cheese thinly and lay over the leeks. Cover with the remaining potatoes, overlapping them in lines for the top layer.

Carefully pour in the cream, then dot with the remaining butter. Cook in a preheated oven, 200°C, 400°F, Gas Mark 6 for about 1½ hours, until the potatoes are soft and golden.

SERVES 4

Nutritional content per serving: Carbohydrate: 46 Fat: 38 Fibre: 5 Kilocalories: 580

SPINACH PANCAKES WITH WILD MUSHROOMS

THE FLAVOUR OF THE MUSHROOM FILLING IS GREATLY IMPROVED BY THE ADDITION OF DRIED CEP MUSHROOMS, KNOWN AS PORCINI IN ITALIAN. IF UNAVAILABLE USE CHESTNUT MUSHROOMS

BATTER:
- 125 g (4 oz) frozen spinach, defrosted
- 125 g (4 oz) plain flour
- 300 ml (½ pint) milk
- 1 egg
- 1 tablespoon sunflower oil
- ground nutmeg
- salt and pepper
- button mushrooms

FILLING:
- 25 g (1 oz) dried cep mushrooms or 50 g (2 oz) chestnut mushrooms
- 2 tablespoons olive oil
- 1 onion, chopped
- 1 clove garlic, chopped
- 250 g (8 oz) button mushrooms, quartered
- 1 tablespoon wholemeal plain flour
- 2 tablespoons double cream
- 50 g (2 oz) Mozzarella cheese, grated
- chervil sprigs to garnish

Press the spinach to extract excess water and put into a blender or food processor with the remaining batter ingredients, seasoning to taste. Blend until smooth, then pour into a jug and leave to stand for 30 minutes. Cook the pancakes as instructed on page 34.

To make the filling, pour boiling water over the dried mushrooms to cover and leave to soak for 30 minutes. Drain and reserve the liquid. Chop the mushrooms. Heat the oil in a pan and fry the onion until softened, add the garlic, button mushrooms and dried or chestnut mushrooms and cook for 2 minutes, stirring occasionally. Stir in the flour, then add 125 ml (4 fl oz) of the reserved mushroom liquid or water and stir continuously until thickened. Stir in the cream with seasoning to taste. Put a tablespoon of the mushroom mixture on each pancake, roll up and place in a greased, shallow, ovenproof dish. Sprinkle with the cheese and bake in a preheated oven, 190°C, 370°F, Gas Mark 5 for 15 minutes until heated through. Garnish with the chervil sprigs and serve.

SERVES 4

Nutritional content per serving: Carbohydrate: 35 Fat: 23 Fibre: 6 Kilocalories: 400

Spinach Pancakes with Wild Mushrooms; Leek and Potato Gratin

SPICED POTATO AND SPINACH

3 tablespoons sunflower oil
1 onion, sliced
2 cloves garlic, chopped
2.5 cm (1 inch) piece fresh root ginger, chopped finely
1 tablespoon black mustard seeds
1 teaspoon cumin seeds
1 tablespoon ground coriander
1/4 teaspoon chilli powder
125 g (4 oz) green lentils
350 ml (12 fl oz) water or vegetable stock
500 g (1 lb) potatoes, chopped roughly
500 g (1 lb) frozen leaf spinach, defrosted and chopped roughly
salt and pepper

Heat the oil in a flameproof casserole and fry the onion until softened. Add the garlic, ginger and all the spices and fry gently for 1–2 minutes, stirring constantly. Add the lentils and stir well until coated in the spices, then add the water or stock, cover and cook for 15 minutes. Mix in the potato and spinach with seasoning to taste.

Cover and cook very gently for 55–60 minutes, stirring occasionally and adding more water if it becomes too dry.

Freezing: is recommended. Turn into a rigid freezerproof container, cover, seal and freeze. This will keep for up to 3 months. Defrost overnight in the refrigerator or at room temperature for 4 hours.

SERVES 4

Nutritional content per serving: Carbohydrate: 48 Fat: 12 Fibre: 6 Kilocalories: 340

VEGETABLE COUSCOUS

COUSCOUS IS A SORT OF HARD WHEAT SEMOLINA WHICH HAS BEEN GROUND, DAMPENED AND ROLLED IN FLOUR. IT IS WIDELY USED IN NORTH AFRICAN COUNTRIES AND HAS GIVEN ITS NAME TO A DISH COMPOSED OF THE COUSCOUS GRAIN AND A DELICIOUS VEGETABLE STEW WHICH ACCOMPANIES IT. BULGAR WHEAT IS A GOOD ALTERNATIVE

2 tablespoons olive oil
2 onions, sliced
1 teaspoon ground cinnamon
1 teaspoon turmeric
1 teaspoon ground ginger
1/2 teaspoon chilli powder
2 cloves garlic, crushed
2 carrots, quartered
2 parsnips, cut into fingers
125 g (4 oz) broad beans
1 × 432 g (15 oz) can chickpeas, drained
2 tablespoons tomato purée
600 ml (1 pint) vegetable stock
375 g (12 oz) couscous
50 g (2 oz) dates, stoned
2 courgettes, sliced
125 g (4 oz) green beans, cut into 2.5 cm (1 inch) lengths
4 tomatoes, skinned and cut into 8 wedges
2 tablespoons chopped parsley
2 tablespoons blanched almonds, toasted
salt and pepper

Heat the oil in a large saucepan, over which you can later fit a steamer. Add the onions to the pan and fry gently until softened. Add the spices and garlic and cook for 1 minute.

Add the carrots, parsnips, broad beans, chickpeas and tomato purée with the stock, bring to the boil, add seasoning to taste and cook for 20 minutes.

Meanwhile, put the couscous into a bowl, cover with water and leave to soak for 15 minutes. Drain thoroughly, mix in the dates and put into a steamer or colander, lined with muslin.

Add the courgettes, green beans, tomatoes and parsley to the vegetables and stir well. Fit the steamer or colander over the saucepan, making sure the bottom does not touch the stew. Steam, uncovered, for 20 minutes, until the vegetables are tender and the couscous is heated through.

Turn the couscous on to a large, round serving dish and separate the grains with a fork. Ladle on a little broth to moisten it, and shape into a mound. Lift out the vegetables, place over the mound of couscous and sprinkle with the almonds. Serve the remaining broth in a separate bowl.

SERVES 4

Nutritional content per serving: Carbohydrate: 120 Fat: 18 Fibre: 18 Kilocalories: 715

Spiced Potato and Spinach; Vegetable Couscous (bottom); Spiced Cauliflower with Coconut

SPICED CAULIFLOWER WITH COCONUT

1 cauliflower, divided into florets
2 tablespoons sunflower oil
1 onion, sliced
2.5 cm (1 inch) piece fresh root ginger, chopped
2 cloves garlic, chopped
175 g (6 oz) okra, tops removed
2 teaspoons ground coriander
1 teaspoon ground cumin
1 teaspoon ground turmeric
25 g (1 oz) creamed coconut
200 ml (5 fl oz) water or vegetable stock
75 g (3 oz) natural yogurt
1 teaspoon cornflour
1 teaspoon chopped coriander
salt and pepper

Blanch the cauliflower in boiling salted water for 2 minutes then drain and set aside.

Heat the oil in a pan and fry the onion until softened. Add the ginger, garlic and okra and fry, stirring, for 2 minutes. Add the spices and cook for a further 1 minute. Blend the coconut with the water or stock until smooth, then add to the pan with the cauliflower and seasoning to taste. Cover and simmer over a low heat for 8–10 minutes until tender.

Blend the yogurt with the cornflour. Remove the cauliflower from the heat and mix in the yogurt and coriander. Serve with basmati rice and puppadoms.

SERVES 4

Nutritional content per serving: Carbohydrate: 7 Fat: 10 Fibre: 4 Kilocalories: 135

SPRING ROLLS WITH TOFU

2 tablespoons soy sauce
1 teaspoon sesame oil
125 g (4 oz) tofu (bean curd), cubed
2 tablespoons sunflower oil
1 leek, cut into julienne strips
1 carrot, cut into julienne strips
75 g (3 oz) mangetout, halved lengthways
2 cloves garlic, chopped
1 teaspoon chopped fresh root ginger
125 g (4 oz) mushrooms, sliced
½ teaspoon five-spice powder
75 g (3 oz) bean sprouts
1 teaspoon cornflour
4 sheets filo pastry
40 g (1½ oz) butter, melted
oil for deep frying
SAUCE:
1 tablespoon tahini paste
1 tablespoon soy sauce
2 tablespoons sesame oil
2 tablespoons dry sherry
radish flowers and spring onion tassels to garnish

Mix the soy sauce and sesame oil with 2 tablespoons of water. Add the tofu to the soy mixture and leave to marinate.

Heat the oil and cook the leek, carrot and mangetout for 2 minutes. Add the garlic, ginger and mushrooms and cook for 3 minutes, stirring frequently, until the vegetables are tender yet crisp.

Remove the tofu from the marinade using a slotted spoon and add to the vegetables, together with the five-spice powder and bean sprouts. Blend the cornflour with the marinade and pour over the vegetables. Cook until thickened.

Cut all the sheets of filo pastry in half across the length to give 8 pieces, about 23 × 34 cm (9 × 14 inches). Cut the pile in half again across the width to give 16 pieces about 23 × 18 cm (9 × 7 inches). Spread one quarter with butter and lay another quarter on top. Spread a spoonful of the vegetable mixture at one end, fold in both sides then roll up. Repeat with the remaining pastry and filling.

To make the sauce, blend the tahini with 2 tablespoons of water then mix in the remaining ingredients.

Heat the oil to 180°C, 350°F or until a cube of bread browns in 30 seconds. Immerse the rolls and cook for 4 minutes, turning once.

Garnish with radish flowers and spring onion tassels and serve with the sauce.

SERVES 4

Nutritional content per serving: Carbohydrate: 11 Fat: 24 Fibre: 3 Kilocalories: 290

TOFU AND SHITAKE STIR-FRY

2 tablespoons soy sauce
2 tablespoons dry sherry
250 g (8 oz) firm tofu (bean curd), sliced
2 tablespoons sunflower oil
50 g (2 oz) cashew nuts
2 cloves garlic, sliced
1 cm (½ inch) piece fresh root ginger, chopped
1 red pepper, cored, deseeded and sliced
125 g (4 oz) mangetout, halved lengthways
175 g (6 oz) shitake mushrooms, sliced
½ teaspoon five-spice powder
125 g (4 oz) bean sprouts
4 spring onions, sliced diagonally
1 teaspoon cornflour
1 tablespoon sesame oil

Mix the soy sauce and sherry together in a bowl, add the tofu and leave for 30 minutes to marinate.

Heat half the sunflower oil in a wok and fry the cashew nuts over a medium heat, stirring until golden. Remove and set aside.

Add the remaining sunflower oil to the wok, add the garlic, ginger, red pepper, mangetout, mushrooms and five-spice powder and stir-fry for 4 minutes. Add the bean sprouts, spring onions and nuts. Stir-fry for 2 minutes. Drain the tofu, blend the marinade with the cornflour, pour over the stir-fried vegetables and stir until the sauce has thickened. Place on a heated serving dish and keep warm.

Heat the sesame oil in the wok. Cook the tofu for 30 seconds on each side, then arrange on the vegetables. Serve with Chinese noodles.

SERVES 4

Nutritional content per serving: Carbohydrate: 10 Fat: 20 Fibre: 2 Kilocalories: 260

VEGETABLE TEMPURA

- 2 carrots, sliced diagonally
- 1 onion, thickly sliced into rings
- 125 g (4 oz) button mushrooms
- 125 g (4 oz) broccoli florets
- 125 g (4 oz) tofu (bean curd), sliced
- 1 sheet nori seaweed or 2 leaves spring greens, cut into wide strips
- oil for deep frying

BATTER:

- 125 g (4 oz) plain flour, sifted
- 2 teaspoons arrowroot
- 250 ml (8 fl oz) carbonated mineral water

DIPPING SAUCE:

- 150 ml (1/4 pint) vegetable stock
- 2 tablespoons light soy sauce
- 2 tablespoons sweet sherry
- 2 teaspoons chopped fresh root ginger
- radish flowers and spring onion tassels to garnish

To make the batter, sift the flour and arrowroot into a bowl, make a well in the centre, and add the water a little at a time, beating well to mix, to form a smooth batter.

To make the dipping sauce, put the stock, soy sauce, sherry and ginger into a small saucepan and heat gently.

Heat the oil to 170°C, 325°F. It is ready when a drop of batter immediately rises to the surface.

Make sure all the vegetables are dry. Dip into the batter, a few at a time, and shake to remove excess. Deep fry for about 3 minutes, until crisp. Continue until all the ingredients are cooked. Drain on kitchen paper, garnish with radish flowers and spring onion tassels and serve immediately with the warm dipping sauce.

SERVES 4

Nutritional content per serving: Carbohydrate: 40 Fat: 2 Fibre: 5 Kilocalories: 195

Spring Rolls with Tofu; Tofu and Shitake Stir-fry (top left); Vegetable Tempura (bottom); Spring Roll filling (top right)

GRAINS, BEANS AND PULSES

MANY OF THE RECIPES IN THIS BOOK HAVE ORIGINS IN THE MIDDLE AND FAR EAST, WHERE GRAINS AND PULSES ARE SO POPULAR. THE DISHES ARE VERY PALATABLE AS WELL AS WHOLESOME AND IF YOU ARE NOT ACCUSTOMED TO SUCH RECIPES YOU MAY BE IN FOR A VERY PLEASANT GASTRONOMIC EXPERIENCE.

WALNUT AND CUMIN LOAF

IF YOU CANNOT OBTAIN FRESH VINE LEAVES YOU CAN USE PRESERVED VINE LEAVES INSTEAD, REMEMBERING TO RINSE THEM THOROUGHLY BEFORE USE

8 large vine leaves
2 tablespoons olive oil
1 onion, chopped
2 celery sticks, chopped
2 cloves garlic, chopped
1 teaspoon ground coriander
1 teaspoon ground cumin
1 tablespoon wholemeal plain flour
125 ml (4 fl oz) vegetable stock
1 tablespoon tomato purée
125 g (4 oz) walnuts, chopped very finely
125 g (4 oz) fresh wholemeal breadcrumbs
2 tablespoons chopped parsley
1 tablespoon chopped coriander leaves
1 egg
salt and pepper
YOGURT SAUCE:
150 g (5 oz) natural yogurt
1 teaspoon tomato purée
1 teaspoon ground coriander
1 teaspoon clear honey
1 teaspoon cornflour
1 teaspoon chopped fresh coriander

Blanch the vine leaves in boiling water for 3 minutes, drain, rinse in cold water and use to line a 500 g (1 lb) loaf tin.

Heat the oil in a pan, add the onion and celery and fry until softened. Add the garlic and spices and cook for a further minute, then stir in the flour and gradually mix in the stock. Bring to the boil, stirring, and cook until thickened. Add the remaining ingredients and mix together thoroughly.

Turn into the lined loaf tin, fold over any overlapping vine leaves, cover with foil and bake in a preheated oven, 180°C, 350°F, Gas Mark 4 for 1 hour–1 hour 10 minutes.

To make the sauce, mix all the ingredients together and heat very gently. Do not boil or the yogurt will curdle.

Freezing: is recommended. Before cooking, cover with foil and freeze. This will keep for up to 3 months. Defrost overnight in the refrigerator, or for 4 hours at room temperature.

SERVES 4–6

Nutritional content per serving: Carbohydrate: 23 Fat: 26 Fibre: 7 Kilocalories: 360

FASULYE PILAKISI (TURKISH BEAN SALAD)

THIS IS SERVED IN TURKEY AS A MEZZE (AN ASSORTMENT OF HORS D'OEUVRES), BUT IT MAKES A GOOD LUNCHEON DISH, WITH LOTS OF OLIVE BREAD (SEE PAGE 72)

250 g (8 oz) borlotti beans, soaked overnight
3 tablespoons olive oil
1 onion, chopped
2 cloves garlic, chopped
1 carrot, chopped
1 celery stick, chopped
1 potato, chopped
4 tomatoes, skinned and chopped
1 tablespoon tomato purée
salt and pepper
1 tablespoon chopped parsley to garnish

Put the beans into a pan of boiling water and boil for 30 minutes. Drain, reserving the liquid.

Heat the oil in a pan and fry the onion until softened. Add the garlic, carrot, celery and potato and cook for a further 2 minutes. Add the beans, 300 ml (½ pint) of the reserved bean liquid, tomatoes, tomato purée and seasoning to taste. Cover and simmer for 1 hour until the beans are tender.

Allow to cool and serve sprinkled with parsley.

SERVES 4

Nutritional content per serving: Carbohydrate: 37 Fat: 12 Fibre: 18 Kilocalories: 310

Walnut and Cumin Loaf; Fasulye Pilakisi

Cashew Nut and Cranberry Croquettes

5 tablespoons sunflower oil
1 onion, chopped
2 celery sticks, chopped
1 clove garlic, crushed
4 tablespoons wholemeal plain flour
1 x 225 g (7 oz) can chopped tomatoes
50 g (2 oz) cranberries
125 g (4 oz) cashew nuts, finely chopped
125 g (4 oz) wholemeal breadcrumbs
1 tablespoon soy sauce
2 tablespoons chopped parsley
SAUCE:
1 tablespoon sunflower oil
4 spring onions, chopped
1 tablespoon plain flour
1 teaspoon redcurrant jelly
75 ml (3 fl oz) vegetable stock
50 ml (2 fl oz) port
1 teaspoon soy sauce
50 g (2 oz) cranberries
pepper

Heat 2 tablespoons of the oil in a pan and fry the onion until softened. Add the celery and garlic and fry for a further 3 minutes, stirring occasionally. Mix in 2 tablespoons of the flour, add the tomatoes and cook well until thickened, stirring. Add the cranberries, cashew nuts, breadcrumbs, soy sauce and parsley and mix well together.

Divide the mixture into 8 pieces and, using dampened hands, shape into croquettes.

Put the remaining flour into a plastic bag, add the croquettes one at a time and shake well until coated. Fry in the remaining oil for 2 minutes on each side until golden brown and crisp.

To make the sauce, heat the oil in a small pan and fry the white part of the onions for 1 minute. Mix in the flour and redcurrant jelly, then gradually add the stock and port. Bring to the boil, stirring, then add the soy sauce, pepper, cranberries and remaining spring onions and cook for 5 minutes.

Arrange the croquettes on a serving dish and serve the sauce separately.

Freezing: is recommended for the croquettes. Open freeze, then pack into a rigid, freezerproof container, cover, seal and return to the freezer. They will keep for up to 3 months. To defrost, unpack and leave at room temperature for 2 hours.

SERVES 4

Nutritional content per serving: Carbohydrate: 40 Fat: 38 Fibre: 7 Kilocalories: 550

Spiced Bulgar Pilaf

AN IDEAL ACCOMPANIMENT TO SERVE WITH BLACK BEAN PATTIES, SEE RIGHT

175 g (6 oz) bulgar wheat
about 900 ml (1 1/2 pints) boiling water
75 g (3 oz) dried apricots, chopped
3 tablespoons olive oil
1 onion, chopped
3 tablespoons pine kernels
2 cloves garlic, sliced
1 teaspoon ground cumin
1 teaspoon allspice
2 tablespoons chopped parsley
25 g (1 oz) pistachio nuts, shelled and chopped roughly
salt and pepper

Put the bulgar wheat into a bowl and cover with the boiling water, leave to soak for 1 hour. Put the apricots into a separate bowl, cover with boiling water and leave to soak for 1 hour. Drain the bulgar wheat and apricots thoroughly.

Heat the oil in a frying pan and fry the onion until softened. Add the pine kernels and garlic and fry until beginning to turn golden. Add the spices and fry for a further 1 minute.

Add the bulgar, apricots, parsley, pistachio nuts and seasoning to taste and heat through, stirring constantly.

SERVES 4–6

Nutritional content per serving: Carbohydrate: 50 Fat: 15 Fibre: 13 Kilocalories: 375

Cashew Nut and Cranberry Croquettes; Black Bean Patties; Spiced Bulgar Pilaf

Black Bean Patties

BORLOTTI BEANS

250 g (8 oz) black beans, soaked overnight
2 cloves garlic, crushed
½ teaspoon ground cumin
2 teaspoons ground coriander
2 tablespoons chopped fresh coriander
2 tablespoons tomato purée
6 spring onions, chopped finely
3 carrots, grated
50 g (2 oz) wholemeal breadcrumbs
2 tablespoons sunflower oil + 1 EGG
salt and pepper
coriander sprigs to garnish
SOURED CREAM SAUCE:
150 ml (¼ pint) soured cream
1 teaspoon chopped fresh coriander
+ 1 x SPRING ONION.

MIXTURE V. WET; MAYBE LEAVE OUT EGG? OR ADD SOME BREADCRUMBS TO MIXTURE.

Drain the beans. Place in a pan and cover with cold water. Bring to the boil and cook rapidly for 10 minutes then cover and simmer for 45 minutes, adding salt towards the end of the cooking time. Drain well and purée in a blender or food processor. Add the garlic, ground spices, coriander, tomato purée, spring onions, carrots and seasoning and blend again until well mixed.

Shape into 12 patties and shake each one in the breadcrumbs until completely coated. Heat the oil in a frying pan and fry for 3 minutes on each side, then drain on kitchen paper.

To make the sauce, mix the soured cream with the coriander, add seasoning and heat gently. Garnish with coriander sprigs and serve the patties with a little sauce and spiced bulgar pilaf (see left).

Freezing: is recommended. Before frying, open freeze, then wrap in a polythene bag, seal and return to the freezer for up to 3 months. Defrost overnight, or at room temperature for 4 hours.

SERVES 4

Nutritional content per serving: Carbohydrate: 39 Fat: 17 Fibre: 18 Kilocalories: 360

MEXICAN TOSTADAS

3 tablespoons sunflower oil
2 large onions, chopped
2 cloves garlic, sliced
1 teaspoon cumin powder
1/4 teaspoon chilli powder
2 x 432 g (15 oz) cans borlotti beans, drained
150 ml (1/4 pint) vegetable stock
2 teaspoons chopped fresh coriander
8 tostada shells
1 avocado, halved, peeled and sliced
50 g (2 oz) Cheddar cheese, grated
salt and pepper
TOMATO COULIS:
1 tablespoon olive oil
1 clove garlic, crushed
4 tomatoes, skinned and chopped
1 teaspoon tomato purée

Heat the oil in a pan and fry the onions and garlic until golden; add the spices and fry for 1 minute. Remove from the heat, add half the beans and mash with a potato masher. Add the stock to make a creamy sauce, then add the coriander and remaining beans, with seasoning to taste, and cook for 5 minutes.

To make the tomato coulis, heat the oil in a small pan, add the garlic, tomatoes and tomato purée, with seasoning to taste, and cook for 8 minutes until pulpy.

Heat the tostada shells for 5 minutes in a preheated oven, 190°C, 375°F, Gas Mark 5. Place a spoonful of beans on each shell, then a spoonful of tomato coulis on top. Arrange a few slices of avocado on top of each tostada and sprinkle with cheese.

Microwave: Microwave oil, onion and garlic on Full Power for 3 minutes. Add half the beans and mash well. Add the stock, coriander, spices and remaining beans with seasoning to taste. Microwave on Full Power for 4 minutes, stirring once. To make tomato coulis, microwave the oil, garlic, tomatoes and seasoning to taste on Full Power for 3–4 minutes, stirring once. Assemble as above.

MAKES 8

Nutritional content per serving: Carbohydrate: 25 Fat: 14 Fibre: 8 Kilocalories: 265

LENTIL CHILLI

2 tablespoons sunflower oil
2 onions, chopped
2 celery sticks, sliced
2 cloves garlic, chopped
1 teaspoon paprika
1/4–1/2 teaspoon chilli powder
175 g (6 oz) green lentils
2 tablespoons tomato purée
1 x 380 g (14 oz) can chopped tomatoes
600 ml (1 pint) vegetable stock or water
1 red pepper, cored, deseeded and chopped
1 x 425 g (15 oz) can red kidney beans, drained
2 tablespoons chopped coriander or parsley
salt
chopped parsley to garnish

Heat the oil in a large pan and fry the onions and celery until softened. Add the garlic, paprika and chilli powder and fry for a further 1 minute.

Add the lentils, tomato purée, tomatoes, stock or water and red pepper with seasoning to taste. Cover and cook gently for 45 minutes.

Add the kidney beans and parsley and cook for a further 10 minutes until the lentils are tender.

Sprinkle with chopped parsley and serve with brown rice and a bowl of natural yogurt.

Freezing: is recommended. Pour into a rigid freezerproof container, cover, seal and freeze. This will keep for up to 3 months. Defrost overnight in the refrigerator or at room temperature for 4 hours.

SERVES 4

Nutritional content per serving: Carbohydrate: 48 Fat: 9 Fibre: 16 Kilocalories: 340

Mexican Tostadas; Lentil Chilli

Curried Lentilburgers

4 tablespoons sunflower oil
1 onion, chopped
1 celery stick, chopped
2 cloves garlic, crushed
1 tablespoon curry powder
50 g (2 oz) long-grain brown rice
600 ml (1 pint) water or vegetable stock
175 g (6 oz) red lentils
50 g (2 oz) wholemeal breadcrumbs
1 tablespoon chopped fresh coriander
3 tablespoons wholemeal flour
salt and pepper
coriander sprigs to garnish
SAUCE:
1 tablespoon sunflower oil
1 clove garlic
1/2 teaspoon ground cumin
1/4 teaspoon turmeric
150 g (5 oz) natural yogurt
1 tablespoon chopped fresh coriander

Heat 1 tablespoon of the oil in a pan, add the onion and celery and cook until softened. Add the garlic and curry powder and cook for a further minute, stirring continuously. Add the rice and water or stock, bring to the boil, cover and simmer for 20 minutes. Add the lentils, cover and cook for a further 20–25 minutes, stirring occasionally, then leave to cool, covered. Mix in the breadcrumbs and coriander and season to taste. Using dampened hands, shape the mixture into small balls, then flatten slightly and roll in the flour.

To make the sauce, heat the oil in a small pan and fry the garlic, cumin and turmeric for 1 minute. Remove from the heat, cool slightly and stir in the yogurt and coriander, with seasoning to taste. Reheat gently, being careful not to boil or the yogurt will curdle.

Pour the remaining oil into a frying pan to a depth of 5 mm (1/4 inch) and heat gently. When hot, add the burgers and fry for 3 minutes on each side until crisp and golden brown. Garnish with coriander and serve with the warm sauce.

SERVES 4

Nutritional content per serving: Carbohydrate: 52 Fat: 20 Fibre: 8 Kilocalories: 445

Bulgar Stuffed Tomatoes

2 extra large tomatoes
25 g (1 oz) bulgar wheat
about 300 ml (1/2 pint) boiling water
2 tablespoons safflower oil
1 onion, chopped
2 tablespoons pine kernels
2 cloves garlic, chopped
1 teaspoon ground cumin
2 tablespoons currants
2 tablespoons chopped parsley
salt and pepper

Cut the tomatoes in half, scoop out the pulp with a teaspoon, chop and set aside. Turn the tomatoes upside down and leave to drain on kitchen paper.

Put the bulgar wheat into a bowl. Pour over the water and leave to soak for 30 minutes. Tip the wheat into a strainer lined with muslin to extract as much water as possible.

Heat the oil in a pan and fry the onion until softened. Add the pine kernels, garlic and cumin and fry for 1 minute. Add all the remaining ingredients, with the chopped tomato pulp, and stir thoroughly to mix.

Spoon the mixture into the tomato halves and place in a greased, shallow, ovenproof dish. Bake in a preheated oven, 180°C, 350°F, Gas Mark 4 for 20 minutes. Serve with a mixed green salad.

SERVES 4

Nutritional content per serving: Carbohydrate: 14 Fat: 12 Fibre: 3 Kilocalories: 180

Curried Lentilburgers; Bulgar Stuffed Tomatoes (bottom); Barley Hot Pot

BARLEY HOT POT

YOU CAN USE POT BARLEY FOR THIS, WHICH STILL RETAINS ITS HUSK AND VALUABLE FIBRE; ONCE THAT IS REMOVED IT IS CALLED PEARL BARLEY

2 tablespoons sunflower oil
2 onions, sliced
2 cloves garlic, chopped
3 celery sticks, sliced
3 carrots, sliced
1 small swede, chopped
2 leeks, sliced
750 ml (1¼ pints) water
1 x 400 g (14 oz) can chopped tomatoes
75 g (3 oz) pearl barley
2 tablespoons chopped parsley
2 strips kombu seaweed, halved lengthways (optional)
750 g (1½ lb) potatoes, sliced
salt and pepper

Heat the oil in a large flameproof casserole and fry the onions until softened.

Add the garlic, celery, carrots, swede and leeks with the water, tomatoes and barley. Stir well to mix, adding seasoning to taste. Bring to the boil and simmer for 15 minutes.

Stir in the parsley and kombu, if using, and lay overlapping slices of potato all over the top. Cover and bake in a preheated oven, 180°C, 350°F, Gas Mark 4 for 1½ hours.

Remove the lid, brush with oil and cook for a further 30 minutes.

SERVES 4

Nutritional content per serving: Carbohydrate: 67 Fat: 8 Fibre: 11 Kilocalories: 360

Lentil and spinach au gratin

2 tablespoons sunflower oil
2 onions, chopped
1 clove garlic, chopped
2 teaspoons ground cumin
250 g (8 oz) green lentils
2 carrots, sliced
300 ml (½ pint) tomato juice
1 bay leaf
600 ml (1 pint) vegetable stock or water
500 g (1 lb) frozen spinach, defrosted and chopped roughly
salt and pepper
TOPPING:
25 g (1 oz) fresh wholemeal breadcrumbs
1 tablespoon chopped chives
25 g (1 oz) Cheddar cheese, grated

Heat the oil in a heavy-based pan and fry the onions until softened. Add the garlic and cumin and fry for a further minute. Add the lentils, carrots, tomato juice, bay leaf, stock or water and seasoning to taste, cover, and cook for 30 minutes. Add the spinach and cook for a further 20–30 minutes until the lentils are soft. Turn into a shallow flameproof dish.

To make the topping, mix the breadcrumbs, chives and cheese together and sprinkle over the lentil mixture. Place under a preheated grill for 5 minutes until brown and serve with a salad.

Freezing: is recommended for the lentil mixture before adding the topping. Turn into a rigid, freezerproof container, cover, and freeze. This will keep for up to 3 months. To defrost, put in the refrigerator overnight, or leave at room temperature for 4 hours.

SERVES 4

Nutritional content per serving: Carbohydrate: 46 Fat: 11 Fibre: 10 Kilocalories: 355

Spiced chickpeas

250 g (8 oz) chickpeas, soaked overnight
2 tablespoons sunflower oil
1 onion, sliced
2 cloves garlic, chopped
2 teaspoons chopped fresh root ginger
1 tablespoon ground coriander
2 teaspoons ground cumin
¼ teaspoon chilli powder
2 carrots, sliced
125 g (4 oz) okra, tops removed
1 × 400 g (14 oz) can chopped tomatoes
1 tablespoon chopped fresh coriander
3 tablespoons natural yogurt
salt and pepper
coriander sprigs to garnish

Drain the chickpeas, put into a saucepan and cover with cold water. Bring to the boil and cook vigorously for 10 minutes, then reduce to a simmer and cook for about 1 hour. Drain and reserve 150 ml (¼ pint) of the liquid.

Heat the oil in a heavy-based pan and fry the onion until softened. Add the garlic, ginger and spices, and cook for 2 minutes. Add the carrots, okra, tomatoes, reserved liquid and seasoning to taste. Cover and simmer gently for 1 hour.

Stir in the coriander and yogurt, garnish with coriander sprigs and serve.

Microwave: Microwave chickpeas with boiling water to cover on Full Power for 10 minutes. Stir, cover and microwave on Medium Power for 20–25 minutes. Drain and reserve 150 ml (¼ pint) liquid. Prepare vegetable mixture as above, place in a covered dish and microwave on Full Power for 25 minutes.

SERVES 4

Nutritional content per serving: Carbohydrate: 40 Fat: 11 Fibre: 13 Kilocalories: 310

Lentil and Spinach au Gratin; Spiced Chickpeas (bottom); Spiced Courgette Dhal

SPICED COURGETTE DHAL

- 2 tablespoons safflower oil
- 2 onions, sliced
- 2 cloves garlic, sliced
- 2.5 cm (1 inch) piece fresh root ginger, chopped finely
- 2 teaspoons cumin powder
- 2 teaspoons turmeric
- 2 teaspoons ground coriander
- 300 g (10 oz) moong dhal or green lentils
- 2 celery sticks, sliced
- 1 tablespoon tomato purée
- 1.25 litres (2 pints) vegetable stock
- 4 courgettes, sliced
- 4 tomatoes, skinned and chopped
- 2 tablespoons chopped fresh coriander
- salt and pepper

Heat the oil in a casserole and fry the onions until softened. Add the garlic, ginger and spices and fry for a further 1 minute.

Add the moong dhal or green lentils and celery with the tomato purée, stock and seasoning. Cover and cook for 30 minutes.

Add the courgettes, tomatoes and coriander and cook for a further 30 minutes, stirring occasionally.

Serve with naan bread or chuppatis.

Freezing: is recommended. Turn into a rigid, freezerproof container, cover and freeze. This will keep for up to 3 months. Defrost overnight in the refrigerator or at room temperature for 4 hours.

SERVES 4

Nutritional content per serving: Carbohydrate: 23 Fat: 26 Fibre: 12 Kilocalories: 340

SALADS

SALADS, ELABORATE OR SIMPLE, SHOULD ALWAYS BE FRESH, COLOURFUL AND APPETIZING. THEY ARE A RICH SOURCE OF VITAMINS AND MINERALS SO PLAY AN IMPORTANT PART IN THE VEGETARIAN DIET. USE FRESH HERBS IN ABUNDANCE AND EXPERIMENT WITH EDIBLE FLOWERS SUCH AS PANSIES AND NASTURTIUMS.

Marinated Courgette and Bean Salad

250 g (8 oz) green beans
375 g (12 oz) courgettes, sliced
1 x 432 g (15 oz) can blackeye beans, drained
4 tablespoons olive oil
2 tablespoons lemon juice
1 clove garlic, crushed
2 tablespoons chopped parsley
salt and pepper

Cut the beans into 2.5 cm (1 inch) lengths and cook in boiling salted water for 5 minutes. Add the courgettes and cook for a further 5 minutes. Drain thoroughly and place in a bowl with the blackeye beans.

Add the remaining ingredients with seasoning to taste while still warm and stir well to mix. Leave to cool and serve with crusty bread.

SERVES 4

Nutritional content per serving: Carbohydrate: 22 Fat: 16 Fibre: 12 Kilocalories: 255

Chèvre and Croûton Salad

100 g (3½ oz) roll goat's cheese
1 packet mixed leaf salad
2 heads chicory, sliced diagonally
handful watercress or rocket leaves
2 slices wholemeal bread, crusts removed
4 tablespoons sunflower oil
2 cloves garlic, sliced
FRENCH DRESSING:
3 tablespoons olive oil
2 teaspoons sherry vinegar
1 teaspoon coarse grain mustard
salt and pepper

Cut the goat's cheese into 1 cm (½ inch) slices and lay on a piece of foil on a grill rack. Put all the salad leaves in a bowl. Cut the bread into even-sized cubes, about 1 cm (½ inch) square.

Heat the oil in a frying pan, add the bread cubes and cook, stirring occasionally, until they begin to turn brown. Add the garlic and continue to cook until the croûtons are golden brown. Remove and drain on kitchen paper.

Put the olive oil, vinegar, mustard and seasoning to taste into a screw-top jar and shake vigorously to mix. Pour over the salad and toss thoroughly, then arrange on 4 individual plates.

Put the goat's cheese under a preheated grill for 1–2 minutes, until melting, and place one slice on each salad, then sprinkle with the croûtons and serve immediately.

SERVES 4

Nutritional content per serving: Carbohydrate: 8 Fat: 33 Fibre: 2 Kilocalories: 350

Carrot and Celeriac Salad

375 g (12 oz) celeriac, cut into julienne strips
250 g (8 oz) carrots, cut into julienne strips
125 g (4 oz) natural yogurt
2 tablespoons coarse grain mustard
½ tablespoon creamed horseradish
2 tablespoons chopped parsley

Blanch the celeriac and carrot strips in boiling salted water for 3 minutes. Drain well and leave to cool.

Mix the yogurt, mustard, horseradish and parsley together in a bowl. Tip in the vegetables and toss thoroughly with 2 forks.

Turn into a shallow serving dish.

SERVES 4

Nutritional content per serving: Carbohydrate: 7 Fibre: 6 Kilocalories: 50

Chèvre and Croûton Salad; Marinated Courgette and Bean Salad (top); Carrot and Celeriac Salad

Wild Rice and Walnut Salad

Technically wild rice is not a rice at all, but comes from a wild aquatic grass native to North America. As it has to be gathered by hand, from a boat, it is extremely expensive

25 g (1 oz) wild rice
75 g (3 oz) long-grain brown rice
3 celery sticks, sliced
50 g (2 oz) walnut pieces, chopped
2 tablespoons chives
DRESSING:
2 tablespoons walnut oil
1 tablespoon sherry vinegar
1 teaspoon clear honey
salt and pepper

Cook the wild rice in boiling salted water for 10 minutes. Add the brown rice and cook for a further 30–40 minutes until tender. Drain, rinse and drain again thoroughly.

Mix all the dressing ingredients together in a screw-top jar and shake vigorously to mix.

Put the rice into a bowl with the celery, walnuts and chives, pour over the dressing and mix together thoroughly. Turn into a shallow serving dish.

Microwave: Place the wild rice in a bowl with 450 ml (3/4 pint) boiling water. Cover and microwave on Full Power for 5 minutes. Add the brown rice, cover and microwave on Full Power for 3 minutes. Reduce the power level to Medium and microwave for a further 25 minutes. Drain, rinse and drain again. Prepare the dressing and the salad as above.

SERVES 4

Nutritional content per serving: Carbohydrate: 23 Fat: 15 Fibre: 2 Kilocalories: 230

Oriental Tofu Salad

If you prefer you could substitute smoked tofu instead of the natural variety

175 g (6 oz) firm tofu (bean curd)
3 tablespoons sunflower oil
2 teaspoons soy sauce
1 teaspoon lemon juice
1 clove garlic, crushed
1 cm (1/2 inch) piece fresh root ginger, chopped finely
salt and pepper
1 bunch watercress
125 g (4 oz) bean sprouts
1 small red pepper, cored, deseeded and sliced finely
4 spring onions, sliced diagonally
1 tablespoon sesame seeds

Cut the tofu into small cubes and put in a bowl. Mix the oil, soy sauce, lemon juice, garlic, ginger and seasoning together until blended, pour over the tofu and leave for 15 minutes.

Mix the watercress and bean sprouts together in a bowl. Add the red pepper to the bowl with the onions, tofu and dressing.

Toss until well coated with dressing, turn into a shallow serving dish and sprinkle with the sesame seeds.

SERVES 4

Nutritional content per serving: Carbohydrate: 4 Fat: 15 Fibre: 3 Kilocalories: 175

Oriental Tofu Salad; Wild Rice and Walnut Salad (top); Sesame Coleslaw

SESAME COLESLAW

THE SUCCESS OF COLESLAW DEPENDS VERY MUCH ON THE CABBAGE BEING VERY FINELY SHREDDED. YOU MAY FIND USING A MANDOLINE EASIER THAN PUTTING CABBAGE DOWN THE TUBE OF A FOOD PROCESSOR OR SHREDDING BY HAND

250 g (8 oz) Dutch cabbage, shredded finely
75 g (3 oz) bean sprouts
2 celery sticks, sliced finely
1 red pepper, cored, deseeded and cut into strips
2 tablespoons chopped parsley to garnish
DRESSING:
1 tablespoon tahini paste
1 small clove garlic, crushed
1 tablespoon cider vinegar
1 tablespoon apple juice
1 tablespoon dry sherry
1 teaspoon sesame oil
1 teaspoon soy sauce

Put the cabbage in a large bowl with the bean sprouts, celery and red pepper.

Put the tahini in a bowl with the garlic and gradually mix in the vinegar and apple juice to make a smooth paste. Add the remaining ingredients and mix well.

Pour over the salad and mix together thoroughly, then turn into a serving bowl. Sprinkle with the parsley.

SERVES 4

Nutritional content per serving: Carbohydrate: 5 Fat: 3 Fibre: 4 Kilocalories: 65

Sprouted Lentil Salad; Warm Potato and Dill Salad (top left); Curried Butter Bean Salad (bottom right); Spiced Bulgar Wheat Salad (top right)

Sprouted Lentil Salad

LENTILS WILL TAKE 3–4 DAYS TO GIVE A 1 CM (½ INCH) SPROUT AND WILL DOUBLE THEIR WEIGHT IN THIS TIME

125 g (4 oz) green lentils, sprouted
4 spring onions, chopped
4 large tomatoes, chopped
2 celery sticks, sliced
250 g (8 oz) peas, cooked
2 tablespoons chopped parsley
DRESSING:
3 tablespoons sunflower oil
1 tablespoon cider vinegar
1 tablespoon light soy sauce
1 clove garlic, crushed
salt and pepper

To make the dressing, put all the ingredients together in a screw-top jar and shake vigorously until emulsified.

Put the sprouted lentils in a bowl, pour on the dressing and leave to marinate for 15 minutes. Add the onions, tomatoes, celery, peas and parsley, toss thoroughly and serve.

SERVES 6

Nutritional content per serving: Carbohydrate: 6 Fat: 8 Fibre: 6 Kilocalories: 100

WARM POTATO AND DILL SALAD

TO MAKE THIS A MORE SUBSTANTIAL SALAD YOU CAN ADD 3 HARD-BOILED EGGS

750 g (1½ lb) waxy potatoes, peeled
2 tablespoons French dressing (see page 61)
4 spring onions, chopped
3 dill pickles, chopped
2 tablespoons chopped dill
75 ml (3 fl oz) soured cream

Cook the potatoes in boiling salted water until tender. Drain well, chop roughly and place in a mixing bowl. Pour over the dressing and mix well to coat.

Add all the remaining ingredients, mix thoroughly, turn into a shallow serving dish and serve warm.

SERVES 4–6

Nutritional content per serving: Carbohydrate: 38 Fat: 10 Fibre: 2 Kilocalories: 240

SPICED BULGAR WHEAT SALAD

175 g (6 oz) bulgar wheat
about 900 ml (1½ pint) boiling water
3 tablespoons olive oil
1 onion, chopped
75 g (3 oz) pine kernels
1 teaspoon ground cumin
1 teaspoon ground coriander
4 tomatoes, deseeded and chopped
2 tablespoons tomato purée
1 tablespoon chopped mint
1 tablespoon chopped parsley
2 tablespoons lemon juice
salt and pepper

Soak the bulgar wheat in the boiling water for 30 minutes. Tip the wheat into a strainer lined with muslin then squeeze the muslin to extract as much water as possible.

Heat the oil in a pan and fry the onion until softened, add pine kernels and cook until beginning to brown. Add the spices and fry for 1 minute. Add the bulgar wheat with all the remaining ingredients and stir thoroughly until well mixed.

Freezing: is recommended only for the onion, bulgar wheat and spices. Freeze in freezerproof container; this will keep for up to 3 months. Defrost overnight in a refrigerator or at room temperature for 4 hours, then add the tomatoes, tomato purée, herbs, lemon juice and seasoning.

SERVES 6–8

Nutritional content per serving: Carbohydrate: 35 Fat: 12 Fibre: 4 Kilocalories: 230

CURRIED BUTTER BEAN SALAD

1 small cauliflower, broken into small florets
1 tablespoon sunflower oil
1 onion, chopped
2 teaspoons curry powder
150 g (5 oz) natural yogurt
1 teaspoon clear honey
1 X 432 g (15 oz) can butter beans, drained
1 tablespoon chopped coriander
salt

Blanch the cauliflower in boiling salted water for 4 minutes, then drain well and put into a bowl.

Heat the oil in a pan and fry the onion until softened. Add the curry powder and fry for a further 1 minute. Cool slightly, then stir in the yogurt and honey with salt to taste.

Tip the curry mixture over the cauliflower, add the butter beans and coriander, and mix together. Turn into a bowl to serve.

SERVES 4–6

Nutritional content per serving: Carbohydrate: 19 Fat: 4 Fibre: 6 Kilocalories: 145

FRESH DATE AND APPLE SALAD

2 russet apples, quartered and cored
4 tablespoons natural yogurt
4 tablespoons mayonnaise
175 g (6 oz) fresh dates
4 celery sticks, chopped
50 g (2 oz) raisins
50 g (2 oz) hazelnuts, chopped and toasted
3 tablespoons chopped parsley

Chop the apples roughly and put into a bowl with the yogurt and mayonnaise. Mix well to coat the apples so that they do not go brown.

Cut the dates in half lengthways, remove the stone, then cut in half again. Add to the bowl with the remaining ingredients and mix together thoroughly.

SERVES 6

Nutritional content per serving: Carbohydrate: 32 Fat: 17 Fibre: 5 Kilocalories: 280

AVOCADO AND CHICORY SALAD

2 avocados, halved and stoned
2 oranges
2 heads chicory
125 g (4 oz) lamb's lettuce, washed
1 tablespoon pine kernels, toasted
basil sprigs to garnish
LEMON DRESSING:
3 tablespoons olive oil
2 tablespoons lemon juice
1 tablespoon clear honey
salt and pepper

Peel the avocados and slice into a bowl. Shake all the dressing ingredients together in a screw-top jar, pour over the avocado and toss until completely coated.

Remove the peel and pith from the oranges and cut into segments, holding the fruit over the bowl so that any juice is included.

Cut the chicory diagonally across into 1 cm (½ inch) slices and add to the bowl with the lamb's lettuce. Toss together thoroughly and sprinkle with the pine kernels and garnish with basil sprigs.

SERVES 4–6

Nutritional content per serving: Carbohydrate: 10 Fat: 12 Fibre: 2 Kilocalories: 145

CAULIFLOWER AND SESAME SALAD

THE FLAVOUR OF THE CAULIFLOWER IS ENHANCED IF IT IS BLANCHED, BUT IF YOU PREFER YOU CAN USE IT RAW TO GIVE A MORE CRUNCHY SALAD. USE GREEN LENTILS FOR SPROUTING – THEY TAKE ABOUT 2 DAYS

1 small cauliflower divided into florets
75 g (3 oz) green lentil sprouts
1 bunch watercress
1 tablespoon sesame seeds
DRESSING:
2 tablespoons tahini paste
1 clove garlic, crushed
2 tablespoons cider vinegar
2 tablespoons apple juice
2 tablespoons dry sherry
2 teaspoons sesame oil
2 teaspoons soy sauce

Blanch the cauliflower in boiling salted water for 2 minutes, drain and leave to cool.

Put the tahini in a bowl with the garlic and gradually mix in the vinegar and apple juice to make a smooth paste. Add the remaining dressing ingredients and mix well.

Pour the dressing over the cauliflower, add the lentil sprouts and mix thoroughly to coat. Leave to marinate for 30 minutes. Add the watercress, turn into a serving bowl and sprinkle with the sesame seeds.

SERVES 4–6

Nutritional content per serving: Carbohydrate: 4 Fat: 8 Fibre: 3 Kilocalories: 110

WATERMELON VINAIGRETTE

1 kg (2 lb) watermelon, cut into wedges
1 tablespoon chopped mint
½ cucumber, peeled, halved and sliced thinly
2 tablespoons olive oil
1 tablespoon lemon juice
1 tablespoon sesame seeds, toasted
1 bunch watercress
salt and pepper

Deseed the watermelon and remove the skin. Slice the watermelon thinly, place in a bowl and sprinkle with the mint. Add the cucumber.

Mix the oil, lemon juice and seasoning together, pour over the salad and toss together thoroughly. Place in the centre of a serving dish, sprinkle with sesame seeds and surround with the watercress.

SERVES 6

Nutritional content per serving: Carbohydrate: 6 Fat: 6 Fibre: 3 Kilocalories: 85

Fresh Date and Apple Salad; Avocado and Chicory Salad (bottom); Watermelon Vinaigrette (top); Cauliflower and Sesame Salad

Brown rice and bean salad

125 g (4 oz) long-grain brown rice
1 x 425 g (15 oz) can red kidney beans, drained
1 red pepper, cored, deseeded and diced
2 celery sticks, chopped
4 spring onions, chopped
50 g (2 oz) cashew nuts, toasted
3 tablespoons chopped parsley
DRESSING:
3 tablespoons olive oil
2 teaspoons soy sauce
2 teaspoons sesame oil
1 tablespoon cider vinegar
1 clove garlic, crushed
salt and pepper

Cook the rice in boiling, salted water for 30–40 minutes until tender. Drain, rinse and drain again thoroughly.

Put all the dressing ingredients into a screw-top jar and shake well.

Put the rice into a bowl with the kidney beans, red pepper, celery, onions, nuts and parsley. Pour over the dressing and mix together thoroughly. Turn into a shallow serving dish.

SERVES 4–6

Nutritional content per serving: Carbohydrate: 47 Fat: 21 Fibre: 10 Kilocalories: 405

Potato and spinach salad

625 g (1 1/4 lb) baby new potatoes, scrubbed
175 g (6 oz) spinach
6 tablespoons soured cream
1 clove garlic, crushed
2 tablespoons chopped chives
1 tablespoon lemon juice
1/4 teaspoon grated nutmeg
2 tablespoons milk
salt and pepper

Cook the potatoes in boiling salted water for 15 minutes until tender. Drain well, turn into a serving dish and leave to cool.

Cook the spinach in a little water for 6 minutes, then drain thoroughly and leave to cool. Put into a blender or food processor with the soured cream, garlic, chives, lemon juice, nutmeg and seasoning to taste. Blend to a purée, adding a little milk to thin if necessary, pour over the potatoes and mix thoroughly.

SERVES 4

Nutritional content per serving: Carbohydrate: 32 Fat: 5 Fibre: 3 Kilocalories: 185

Aubergine and yogurt salad

2 aubergines, sliced
75 ml (3 fl oz) olive oil
300 g (10 oz) natural yogurt
1 clove garlic, crushed
2 tablespoons chopped parsley
salt and pepper

Put the aubergines into a colander, sprinkling each layer with salt, and leave to drain for 30 minutes. Rinse well and pat dry.

Heat half the oil in a frying pan and fry the aubergines in 2 batches, on both sides, until golden brown. Mix the yogurt with the garlic, parsley and seasoning to taste. Spoon the yogurt into a shallow serving dish and arrange some aubergines on top. Continue the layers, finishing with yogurt. Serve with pitta bread.

SERVES 4

Nutritional content per serving: Carbohydrate: 10 Fat: 20 Fibre: 4 Kilocalories: 230

Potato and Spinach Salad; Brown Rice and Bean Salad (top left); Aubergine and Yogurt Salad (bottom); Bean Sprout and Mangetout Salad (top right)

BEAN SPROUT AND MANGETOUT SALAD

250 g (8 oz) button mushrooms, sliced
5 tablespoons olive oil
2 teaspoons sesame oil
1 tablespoon soy sauce
1 tablespoon lemon juice
1 clove garlic, chopped
1 teaspoon chopped fresh root ginger
125 g (4 oz) mangetout
1 red pepper, cored, deseeded and sliced finely
175 g (6 oz) bean sprouts
1 tablespoon sesame seeds, toasted
salt and pepper

Slice the mushrooms and put into a bowl. Put the oils, soy sauce, lemon juice, garlic, ginger and seasoning to taste in a small screw-top jar and shake vigorously to mix. Pour over the mushrooms, mix well and leave to marinate for 30 minutes.

Top and tail the mangetout, then cut in half lengthways. Blanch in boiling salted water for 3 minutes, rinse in cold water and drain well. Add to the mushrooms with the red pepper and bean sprouts and toss well again to coat.

Turn into a shallow serving dish and sprinkle with the toasted sesame seeds.

SERVES 4–6

Nutritional content per serving: Carbohydrate: 4 Fat: 24 Fibre: 5 Kilocalories: 253

BAKING

WHOLEMEAL BREAD COULD BE SAID TO BE THE FOUNDATION OF THE VEGETARIAN DIET. IT HAS MORE FLAVOUR THAN WHITE BREAD AND IS A VALUABLE SOURCE OF DIETARY FIBRE. IT IS ALSO BEST TO USE WHOLEMEAL FLOUR IN CAKES AND BISCUITS TO GIVE THEM A RICH FLAVOUR AND MOIST TEXTURE.

Irish Soda Bread

THIS BREAD MUST BE EATEN AS SOON AS POSSIBLE AFTER BAKING, PREFERABLY WHILE STILL WARM. IT IS VERY QUICK TO MAKE AS IT REQUIRES NO PROVING OR KNEADING, SO IT IS IDEAL WHEN YOU RUN OUT OF BREAD. IF YOU HAVE NO BUTTERMILK, YOU CAN EITHER ADD 2 TEASPOONS OF LEMON JUICE TO FRESH MILK OR ADD AN EXTRA TEASPOON OF CREAM OF TARTAR

350 g (12 oz) wholemeal plain flour
1½ teaspoons salt
250 g (8 oz) plain flour
1 teaspoon bicarbonate of soda
1 teaspoon cream of tartar
300 ml (½ pint) buttermilk
4 tablespoons milk
flour for sprinkling

Put the wholemeal flour into a bowl with the salt then sift in the plain flour, bicarbonate of soda and cream of tartar. Add the buttermilk and milk and mix to a soft dough.

Turn on to a floured surface, knead lightly then shape into a 20 cm (8 inch) round about 5 cm (2 inches) thick, and put on to a floured baking sheet. Cut a deep cross on the top of the loaf and sprinkle with flour. Bake in a preheated oven, 220°C, 425°F, Gas Mark 7 for 25–30 minutes. Transfer to a wire rack to cool.

Freezing: is recommended. Wrap in a polythene bag, seal and freeze. This will keep for up to 1 month. To defrost, unwrap and leave at room temperature for 4 hours.

MAKES 1 20 cm (8 inch) LOAF

Nutritional content per serving: Carbohydrate: 45 Fat: 1 Fibre: 4 Kilocalories: 200

Sticky Date Gingerbread

250 g (8 oz) wholemeal plain flour
4 teaspoons ground ginger
2 teaspoons ground cinnamon
1 teaspoon bicarbonate of soda
125 ml (4 fl oz) sunflower oil
50 ml (2 fl oz) black treacle
50 ml (2 fl oz) malt extract
125 g (4 oz) muscovado sugar
250 g (8 oz) dried dates, stoned and chopped
150 ml (¼ pint) apple juice
2 eggs
2 tablespoons sunflower seeds

Grease and line an 18 cm (7 inch) square cake tin. Put the flour into a bowl and sift in the spices and bicarbonate of soda.

Put the oil, black treacle, malt extract, sugar and dates in a saucepan and heat gently until the sugar has completely dissolved. Stir in the apple juice and the eggs, then pour into the dry ingredients and mix together thoroughly.

Pour into the cake tin, sprinkle with sunflower seeds and bake in a preheated oven, 160°C, 325°F, Gas Mark 3 for 1¼ hours until a skewer inserted into the centre comes out clean. Leave in the tin to cool for 5 minutes then turn out on to a wire rack to cool completely.

Freezing: is recommended. Wrap in a polythene bag, seal and freeze. This will keep for up to 3 months. To defrost, unwrap and leave at room temperature for 4 hours.

MAKES 1 × 18 cm (7 inch) SQUARE CAKE

Nutritional content per serving: Carbohydrate: 49 Fat: 4 Fibre: 3 Kilocalories: 310

Irish Soda Bread; Sticky Date Gingerbread

Olive bread

250 g (8 oz) strong plain flour
250 g (8 oz) wholemeal plain flour
1 teaspoon salt
15 g (½ oz) fresh yeast
300 ml (½ pint) warm water
1 tablespoon olive oil
75 g (3 oz) black olives, halved and pitted
2 tablespoons chopped parsley
1 teaspoon sesame seeds

Make the dough as for Granary® Plait, see right. Turn on to a floured surface and knead in the olives and parsley. This will be difficult at first as the olives are oily but after about 5 minutes' kneading they will combine.

Shape into a 23 cm (9 inch) round, flatten slightly and place on a greased baking sheet. Make a cut all the way round the dough 2.5 cm (1 inch) in from the edge. Brush with water and sprinkle with sesame seeds. Cover and leave in a warm place for about 30 minutes until almost doubled in size.

Bake in a preheated hot oven, 220°C, 425°F, Gas Mark 7 for 10 minutes then lower the temperature to 200°C, 400°F, Gas Mark 6 and bake for a further 20 minutes until the bread sounds hollow when tapped underneath.

Freezing: is recommended. Wrap in a polythene bag, seal and freeze. This will keep for up to 1 month. To defrost, unwrap and leave at room temperature for 4 hours.

MAKES 1 × 500 g (1 lb) LOAF

Nutritional content per loaf: Carbohydrate: 366 Fat: 34 Fibre: 39 Kilocalories: 1925

GRANARY® PLAIT

250 g (8 oz) granary® flour
500 g (1 lb) wholemeal plain flour
2 teaspoons salt
15 g (½ oz) fresh yeast
450 ml (¾ pint) warm water
1 tablespoon malt extract
2 tablespoons sunflower oil
1 teaspoon sesame seeds

Mix the flours and salt together in a large bowl. Cream the yeast with a little of the water and leave until frothy. Add to the flours with the remaining water, malt extract and oil and mix thoroughly to a soft dough.

Turn on to a floured surface and knead for 5 minutes until smooth and elastic. Place in a clean bowl, cover with a damp cloth and leave in a warm place to rise for about 2 hours until doubled in bulk.

Turn on to a floured surface and knead for a few minutes, then cut the dough in half. To shape the plait, cut each half into 3 equal pieces. Shape the pieces into long thin 'sausages'. Take 3 'sausages', moisten one end of each with water and press together; plait and dampen the ends to join. Repeat with the remaining dough to make 2 loaves.

Place on baking sheets, brush with water and sprinkle with sesame seeds. Leave to rise in a warm place for 1 hour until doubled in size. Bake in a preheated hot oven, 220°C, 425°F, Gas Mark 7 for 10 minutes, then reduce to 200°C, 400°F, Gas Mark 6 for a further 15–20 minutes until the loaves sound hollow when tapped underneath. Cool on a wire rack.

Microwave: Bread dough proving can be hastened using the microwave. Simply give the dough a short burst of energy during the rising process, then leave to stand for 5–10 minutes before repeating until the dough has risen sufficiently. For the above plait give a 5–10 second burst of microwave energy on Full Power then leave to stand as recommended.

To defrost a frozen plait, microwave on Defrost power for 4 minutes then leave to stand for 5 minutes before slicing.

Freezing: is recommended. Wrap each one in a polythene bag, seal and freeze. These will keep for up to 1 month. To defrost, unwrap and leave at room temperature for about 3 hours.

MAKES 2 LOAVES

Nutritional content per loaf: Carbohydrate: 255 Fat: 23 Fibre: 34 Kilocalories: 1362

Olive Bread; Granary® Plait

RYE AND ONION STICK

- 2 tablespoons sunflower oil
- 1 onion, chopped
- 125 g (4 oz) rye flour
- 350 g (12 oz) wholemeal plain flour
- 1 teaspoon salt
- 15 g (½ oz) fresh yeast
- 300 ml (½ pint) warm water
- 1 teaspoon caraway seeds

Heat the oil in a pan and fry the onion until it is a good brown colour.

Mix the flours and salt together in a bowl. Cream the yeast with a little of the water and leave until frothy. Add to the flour with the remaining water and the fried onions and mix to a soft dough.

Turn on to a floured surface and knead for 5 minutes until smooth and elastic. Place in a clean bowl, cover with a damp cloth and leave in a warm place to rise for about 2 hours until doubled in size.

Turn on to a floured surface and knead for a few minutes, then divide into 2 pieces. Shape into long sticks 35 cm (14 inches) long and place on a greased baking sheet. Make diagonal cuts down the length of the sticks. Brush with water and sprinkle with caraway seeds. Cover and leave in a warm place for about 30–40 minutes until almost doubled in size.

Bake in a preheated oven, 220°C, 425°F, Gas Mark 7, for 10 minutes, then lower the temperature to 200°C, 400°F, Gas Mark 6 and bake for a further 15 minutes or until the sticks sound hollow when tapped underneath. Cool on a wire rack.

Freezing: is recommended. Wrap in a polythene bag, seal and freeze. These will keep for up to 2 months. To defrost, unwrap and leave at room temperature for 2 hours.

MAKES 2

Nutritional content per stick: Carbohydrate: 42 Fat: 6 Fibre: 6 Kilocalories: 230

FIG TEABREAD

- 125 g (4 oz) breakfast bran cereal
- 50 g (2 oz) muscovado sugar
- 150 g (5 oz) dried figs, chopped
- 350 ml (12 fl oz) hot tea
- 125 g (4 oz) wholemeal self-raising flour
- 50 g (2 oz) hazelnuts, chopped and toasted

Grease and line a 500 g (1 lb) loaf tin. Place the bran cereal, sugar, figs and tea in a mixing bowl and leave to soak for 30 minutes. Mix in the flour and all but 1 tablespoon of the nuts and beat thoroughly. Turn into the loaf tin, sprinkle with the remaining nuts and bake in a preheated oven, 180°C, 350°F, Gas Mark 4 for 50–55 minutes. Turn on to a wire rack to cool.

MAKES 1 × 500 g (1 lb) LOAF

Nutritional content per loaf: Carbohydrate: 286 Fat: 27 Fibre: 70 Kilocalories: 1470

Fig Teabread; Rye and Onion Stick (top); Caraway Crackers

CARAWAY CRACKERS

THESE ARE IDEAL TO SERVE WITH CHEESE OR TO NIBBLE WITH DRINKS

50 g (2 oz) wholemeal plain flour
2–3 tablespoons water
1 teaspoon ground cumin
1 teaspoon caraway seeds
1/4 teaspoon salt

Put the flour in a mixing bowl and make a well in the centre. Add the remaining ingredients and mix to a firm dough.

Turn on to a floured surface and knead for 2 minutes until smooth, then leave to rest for 10 minutes.

Cut the dough into 14 pieces and knead into rounds on a floured surface. Roll out thinly and cut into 7 cm (3 inch) circles with a cutter.

Put on baking sheets and cook in a preheated oven, 180°C, 350°F, Gas Mark 4 for 15 minutes, turning over halfway through cooking.

Freezing: is recommended. Put in a rigid freezerproof container, cover, seal and freeze. These will keep for up to 3 months. To defrost, leave at room temperature for 30 minutes.

MAKES 14

Nutritional content per serving: Carbohydrate: 3 Kilocalories: 15

PECAN AND PARSNIP CAKE

300 g (10 oz) wholemeal self-raising flour
2 teaspoons mixed spice
125 g (4 oz) soft brown sugar
175 g (6 oz) raisins
175 g (6 oz) dried dates, stoned and chopped
125 ml (4 fl oz) sunflower oil
1 rounded tablespoon malt extract
2 eggs
175 ml (6 fl oz) milk
250 g (8 oz) parsnips, grated
50 g (2 oz) pecan nuts

Grease and line a 20 cm (8 inch) round cake tin. Put the flour and spice into a mixing bowl, then stir in the sugar, raisins and dates. Make a well in the centre and mix in the oil, malt extract, eggs, milk and parsnips. Beat until well combined.

Turn into the cake tin, arrange the nuts on top, and bake in a preheated oven, 180°C, 350°F, Gas Mark 4 for 1 hour, until a skewer inserted into the centre comes out clean. Turn out on to a wire rack to cool.

Freezing: is recommended. Wrap in a polythene bag, seal and freeze. This will keep for up to 3 months. To defrost, leave at room temperature for 4 hours.

MAKES 1 × 20 cm (8 inch) CAKE

Nutritional content per serving: Carbohydrate: 50 Fat: 14 Fibre: 6 Kilocalories: 335

AMARETTO SPONGE CAKE

125 g (4 oz) soft margarine
75 g (3 oz) caster sugar
2 eggs
200 g (7 oz) wholemeal self-raising flour
150 ml (1/4 pint) milk
75 g (3 oz) ground almonds
1/2 teaspoon almond flavouring
2 tablespoons chopped almonds
SYRUP:
250 g (8 oz) caster sugar
175 ml (6 fl oz) water
2 tablespoons Amaretto liqueur

Grease and line a 20 cm (8 inch) cake tin. Beat the margarine and sugar together until light and fluffy. Beat in the eggs one at a time, adding a tablespoon of flour with the second egg. Fold in the flour alternately with the milk then mix in the ground almonds and almond flavouring.

Turn the mixture into the cake tin, sprinkle with chopped almonds and bake in a preheated oven, 180°C, 350°F, Gas Mark 4 for 40–45 minutes until the centre springs back when lightly pressed.

To make the syrup, put the sugar and water in a small pan and heat gently until dissolved. Cool slightly, then mix in the liqueur.

Make holes all over the surface of the cake with a skewer and gradually pour over the syrup until it is all absorbed.

Freezing: is recommended. Wrap in a polythene bag, seal and freeze. This will keep for up to 3 months. To defrost, unwrap and leave at room temperature for 4 hours.

MAKES 1 × 20 cm (8 in) CAKE

Nutritional content per serving: Carbohydrate: 48 Fat: 18 Fibre: 3 Kilocalories: 375

Amaretto Sponge Cake; Pecan and Parsnip Cake

Granola Crunchies

YOU CAN USE THESE INGREDIENTS TO MAKE GRANOLA BY TURNING THE MIXTURE INTO A LARGE BAKING TIN AND STIRRING OCCASIONALLY DURING COOKING. WHEN COOL, CRUMBLE THE PIECES IN YOUR HAND OR BLEND IN A FOOD PROCESSOR IF YOU LIKE IT FINE. IT'S DELICIOUS FOR BREAKFAST WITH STEWED FRUIT OR YOGURT

125 ml (4 fl oz) safflower oil
75 ml (3 fl oz) malt extract
50 ml (2 fl oz) clear honey
125 g (4 oz) jumbo oats
125 g (4 oz) porridge oats
125 g (4 oz) hazelnuts, chopped
25 g (1 oz) desiccated coconut
25 g (1 oz) sesame seeds

Put the oil, malt extract and honey together in a large pan and heat gently until the malt extract is runny. Add the remaining ingredients and mix together thoroughly. Turn into an 18 × 28 cm (7 × 11 inch) greased baking tin, press to the edges and smooth the top with a palette knife. Bake in a preheated oven, 180°C, 350°F, Gas Mark 4 for 30 minutes. Cool in the tin for 5 minutes, then cut into 18 fingers. Cool completely before removing from the tin.

Freezing: is recommended. Put into a rigid freezerproof container, cover, seal and freeze. These will keep for up to 3 months. To defrost, leave at room temperature for 2 hours.

MAKES 18

Nutritional content per serving: Carbohydrate: 11 Fat: 12 Fibre: 1 Kilocalories: 150

Hazelnutties

75 g (3 oz) soft margarine
75 g (3 oz) soft brown sugar
1 egg
125 g (4 oz) porridge oats
50 g (2 oz) wholemeal plain flour
50 g (2 oz) hazelnuts, chopped and toasted

Cream the margarine and sugar together until light and fluffy. Add the egg and beat thoroughly until thickened, then mix in the porridge oats, flour and hazelnuts.

Roll into balls the size of a walnut, using dampened hands, and place, well apart, on a greased baking sheet. Flatten each ball with a wet palette knife.

Bake in a preheated oven, 190°C, 375°F, Gas Mark 5 for 10–15 minutes until golden brown. Remove to a wire rack to cool.

Microwave: Prepare the mixture as above and shape into balls. Place six in a ring pattern on a large plate or microwave tray and flatten with a wet palette knife. Microwave, six at a time, on Full Power for 2½–3 minutes. Place on a wire rack to cool.

Freezing: is recommended. Pack in a rigid, freezerproof container, cover, seal and freeze. These will keep for up to 3 months. To defrost, remove as many as required and leave at room temperature for 30 minutes.

MAKES 24

Nutritional content per serving: Carbohydrate: 9 Fat: 4 Fibre: 1 Kilocalories: 75

Granola Crunchies; Hazelnutties (bottom); Carob Cookies

CAROB COOKIES

125 g (4 oz) soft margarine
50 g (2 oz) soft brown sugar
grated rind of 1 orange
1 egg
150 g (5 oz) wholemeal self-raising flour
50 g (2 oz) carob bar or plain chocolate, roughly chopped
125 g (4 oz) walnut pieces, chopped

Work the margarine, sugar and orange rind together until creamy. Beat in the egg thoroughly, until thickened, then mix in the flour, carob or chocolate and walnuts.

Put teaspoonfuls of the mixture, well apart, on a greased baking sheet and flatten, using a wet fork.

Bake in a preheated oven, 180°C, 350°F, Gas Mark 4 for 15–20 minutes. Remove to a wire rack to cool.

Freezing: is recommended. Pack in a rigid, freezerproof container, cover, seal and freeze. These will keep for up to 3 months. To defrost, remove as many as required and leave at room temperature for 30 minutes.

MAKES 24

Nutritional content per serving: Carbohydrate: 8 Fat: 8 Fibre: 1 Kilocalories: 95

Walnut tartlets

PÂTE SUCRÉE
125 g (4 oz) plain flour
50 g (2 oz) unsalted butter, softened
50 g (2 oz) caster sugar
2 egg yolks
FILLING:
50 g (2 oz) soft brown sugar
2 tablespoons clear honey
1 tablespoon water
50 g (2 oz) butter
175 g (6 oz) walnut pieces

Sift the flour on to a cool work surface, make a well in the centre and put in the butter, sugar and egg yolks. Using the fingertips of one hand, work the ingredients together, then draw in the flour and work to a paste with the help of a palette knife. Knead lightly until smooth, wrap in a polythene bag and chill for 30 minutes.

Roll the pastry out thinly on a floured surface and use to line 12 patty tins. Press a square of foil into each one and chill for 15 minutes.

Bake blind in a preheated oven, 190°C, 375°F, Gas Mark 5 for 8–10 minutes. Remove the foil and leave to cool.

To make the filling, put the sugar, honey and water into a heavy-based pan and dissolve over a gentle heat. Boil for 5–6 minutes, until a little dropped into cold water forms a soft ball, then remove from the heat and stir in the butter and walnuts. Spoon into the tartlet cases before the filling begins to set.

Leave to cool then remove from the moulds.

MAKES 12

Nutritional content per serving: Carbohydrate: 20 Fat: 13 Fibre: 1 Kilocalories: 230

Hazelnut cake

175 g (6 oz) margarine
175 g (6 oz) soft brown sugar
1 tablespoon malt extract
3 eggs
125 g (4 oz) wholemeal self-raising flour
125 g (4 oz) hazelnuts, ground and toasted
2 tablespoons black coffee
3 tablespoons chopped hazelnuts

Grease and line a 21 cm (8½ inch) round deep cake tin. Cream the margarine and sugar together until light and fluffy, then beat in the malt extract. Beat in the eggs one at a time, adding a tablespoon of flour with the second and third egg.

Fold in the remaining flour, ground hazelnuts and coffee, using a large metal spoon.

Turn into the cake tin, sprinkle with the chopped hazelnuts and bake in a preheated oven, 180°C, 350°F, Gas Mark 4 for 55 minutes to 1 hour until the cake springs back when lightly pressed.

Turn out on to a wire rack to cool.

Freezing: is recommended. Wrap in a polythene bag, seal and freeze. This will keep for up to 3 months. To defrost, leave at room temperature for 4 hours.

MAKES 1 × 21 cm (8½ inch) CAKE

Nutritional content per serving: Carbohydrate: 21 Fat: 28 Fibre: 2 Kilocalories: 310

Walnut Tartlets; Hazelnut Cake (bottom); Banana and Apple Slices

BANANA AND APPLE SLICES

125 g (4 oz) soft margarine
150 g (5 oz) soft brown sugar
2 eggs
275 g (9 oz) wholemeal self-raising flour
2 dessert apples, cored and grated
2 bananas, mashed
75 g (3 oz) sultanas
125 ml (4 fl oz) apple juice
2 tablespoons chopped cashew nuts

Grease and line an 18 × 28 cm (7 × 11 inch) shallow tin. Cream the margarine and sugar together until light and fluffy. Beat in the eggs one at a time, adding a tablespoon of flour with the second egg. Fold in half the flour with the apples, bananas and sultanas. Fold in the remaining flour with the apple juice.

Turn the mixture into the tin and smooth the top with a palette knife. Bake in a preheated oven, 180°C, 350°F, Gas Mark 4 for 45–50 minutes, until the cake springs back when lightly pressed. Turn on to a wire rack to cool, sprinkle with cashew nuts, then cut into slices.

Freezing: is recommended. Pack into a rigid, freezerproof container, cover and freeze. These will keep for up to 3 months. To defrost, remove as many as required and leave at room temperature for 1 hour.

MAKES 20 SLICES

Nutritional content per serving: Carbohydrate: 24 Fat: 7 Fibre: 2 Kilocalories: 160

DESSERTS

THERE ARE SO MANY FRUITS AVAILABLE – THE EXOTIC TROPICAL VARIETIES, THE LUSCIOUS BERRIES OF SUMMER AND THE DUSKY AUTUMNAL FRUITS. THESE MAKE THE SIMPLEST AND HEALTHIEST DESSERTS BUT OCCASIONALLY A RICH CREAMY PUDDING IS THE ORDER OF THE DAY, SO A FEW OF THESE ARE INCLUDED TOO.

SUMMER FRUIT BASKETS

THESE BASKETS ARE IDEAL CONTAINERS FOR ALL SORTS OF FRUITS AND FOOLS. THIS MIXTURE MAKES ABOUT 10, SO YOU CAN KEEP SOME IN THE FREEZER FOR FUTURE USE. BAKE ONLY 3 AT ONE TIME ON A BAKING SHEET, OR THEY WILL SET BEFORE YOU HAVE TIME TO MOULD THEM

BRANDY SNAP BASKETS:
50 g (2 oz) margarine
50 g (2 oz) demerara sugar
50 g (2 oz) golden syrup
50 g (2 oz) plain flour, sifted
FILLING:
125 g (4 oz) raspberries
1 tablespoon caster sugar
2 tablespoons Crème de Framboise liqueur
375 g (12 oz) strawberries, halved
1 tablespoon double cream
strawberry leaves to decorate

Put the margarine, sugar and syrup into a pan and heat gently until the fat has melted, then beat in the flour.

Put 3 spoonfuls of the mixture, well apart, on a baking sheet and press out into 12 cm (5 inch) circles, using dampened fingertips. Bake in a preheated oven, 180°C, 350°F, Gas Mark 4 for 7–10 minutes until golden brown.

Leave to cool slightly, then remove with a palette knife. Mould over a dariole mould or the base of a small tumbler, with the top side of the biscuit to the mould or glass. Leave to set then remove. Repeat with the remaining mixture and biscuits as they cook.

To make the filling, put the raspberries, sugar and liqueur into a blender or food processor and blend until smooth. Sieve to remove the seeds. Put the strawberries into a bowl, pour over two-thirds of the purée and mix together.

Put a spoonful of the remaining purée on each serving plate and swirl to the edges. Put drops of cream on the purée and, using a skewer, mark into an attractive design.

Spoon the filling into the baskets and place one in the centre of each plate. Decorate with strawberry leaves.

Freezing: is recommended for the baskets. Pack into a rigid, freezerproof container, separating the baskets with tissue paper. Cover and freeze. These will keep for up to 3 months. To defrost, unpack and leave at room temperature for 30 minutes.

SERVES 4

Nutritional content per serving: Carbohydrate: 23 Fat: 6 Fibre: 2 Kilocalories: 195

YOGURT WITH FIGS AND PASSION FRUIT

2 passion fruit
250 g (8 oz) Greek yogurt
1 tablespoon clear honey
4 fresh figs
fresh edible leaves to decorate

Cut the passion fruit in half, scoop out the seeds and mix with the yogurt and honey.

Cut each fig into 8 segments, peeling the fruit first if preferred, then fold all but 8 segments into the yogurt mixture.

Spoon the mixture into glass dishes and decorate with the reserved fig segments and fresh leaves.

SERVES 4

Nutritional content per serving: Carbohydrate: 7 Fat: 13 Fibre: 12 Kilocalories: 160

Summer Fruit Baskets; Yogurt with Figs and Passion Fruit

FLOATING ISLANDS

600 ml (1 pint) milk
2 egg whites
2 tablespoons caster sugar
CUSTARD SAUCE:
1½ tablespoons cornflour
3 egg yolks
2 tablespoons caster sugar
2 tablespoons milk
¼ teaspoon vanilla flavouring
CARAMEL:
50 g (2 oz) caster sugar
2 tablespoons hot water

Pour the milk into a shallow ovenproof dish. Whisk the egg whites until stiff, then whisk in the caster sugar.

Use 2 dessertspoons to shape the meringue into 12 small ovals and drop into the milk. Put into a preheated oven, 160°C, 325°F, Gas Mark 3 and bake for 6–8 minutes until firm but not brown. Remove the poached meringue with a fish slice and set aside.

To make the custard, mix the cornflour, egg yolks and sugar together with the cold milk. Tip the poaching milk into a saucepan and bring to the boil, then pour over the egg yolk mixture. Return to the heat and bring to the boil, stirring constantly until thickened. Add the vanilla flavouring, strain into a large bowl, sprinkle with a little caster sugar to prevent a skin forming and leave to cool, then chill for 1 hour.

To make the caramel, put the sugar into a small, heavy-based pan and heat gently until it dissolves into a caramel. Pour in the hot water, shake over the heat until blended, then set aside to cool.

To serve, pour some custard into 4 serving bowls, arrange 3 meringues on top of each, and drizzle the caramel sauce over the top. Use a fine skewer to drag the caramel into a design.

SERVES 4

Nutritional content per serving: Carbohydrate: 42 Fat: 12 Kilocalories: 300

GOOSEBERRY AND ELDERFLOWER JELLY

500 g (1 lb) gooseberries
450 ml (¾ pint) apple juice
4 heads elderflower
75 g (3 oz) caster sugar
1 teaspoon agar agar powder
75 ml (3 fl oz) single cream
6 fresh edible leaves or elderflower sprigs to decorate

Put the gooseberries into a pan with 300 ml (½ pint) of the apple juice and the elderflower heads, tied in muslin. Cover and cook gently, until the gooseberries are soft. Remove the elderflower heads, squeezing out as much juice as possible.

Purée the fruit in a blender or food processor and sieve to remove the tops and tails. Add the sugar and stir until dissolved, then set aside 75 ml (3 fl oz) of the purée.

Put the remaining apple juice into a small pan, sprinkle over the agar agar, and leave to soak for 5 minutes. Bring to the boil and simmer for 3–4 minutes, until dissolved, then add to the gooseberry purée. Turn into 6 × 125 ml (4 fl oz) decorative moulds and chill until set.

To make the sauce, mix the cream with the reserved gooseberry purée. Turn the jellies out on to serving plates, surround each with some sauce, and decorate with the leaves or elderflower sprigs.

SERVES 6

Nutritional content per serving: Carbohydrate: 36 Fat: 4 Fibre: 3 Kilocalories: 120

Gooseberry and Elderflower Jelly; Floating Islands (top); Summer Fruit Platter

SUMMER FRUIT PLATTER

THIS IS ONE OF THE SIMPLEST YET MOST DELICIOUS SUMMER DESSERTS. USE A SELECTION OF FRUITS IN SEASON

150 g (4 oz) raspberries
1 tablespoon clear honey
2 tablespoons Crème de Framboise liqueur
175 g (6 oz) cherries
2 kiwi fruit, peeled and sliced
1 peach, stoned and sliced
125 g (4 oz) redcurrant sprigs
125 g (4 oz) strawberries, sliced

Put the raspberries into a blender or food processor with the honey and blend until smooth. Sieve to remove the seeds then stir in the liqueur and chill.

Put a pool of sauce on one side of each serving plate and arrange the fruits attractively on the other side. Serve with crisp, sweet biscuits.

SERVES 4

Nutritional content per serving: Carbohydrate: 15 Fibre: 7 Kilocalories: 70

Hazelnut and Strawberry Roulade

3 eggs
125 g (4 oz) caster sugar
50 g (2 oz) plain flour, sifted
50 g (2 oz) ground hazelnuts, toasted
1 tablespoon sunflower oil
caster sugar for dredging
FILLING:
250 g (8 oz) double cream
250 g (8 oz) strawberries, chopped
SAUCE:
175 g (6 oz) strawberries
1 tablespoon icing sugar
2 tablespoons double cream

Grease and line a 20 × 30 cm (8 × 12 inch) Swiss roll tin. Whisk the eggs and sugar together until very thick and mousse-like. Carefully fold in the flour and hazelnuts, adding the oil at the last moment.

Turn the mixture into the Swiss roll tin. Bake in a preheated oven, 200°C, 400°F, Gas Mark 6 for 8–10 minutes, until the cake springs back when lightly pressed in the centre.

Wring out a clean tea towel in hot water and lay it on a work surface. Place a sheet of greaseproof paper on top, and sprinkle it with caster sugar. Turn the sponge upside down on the paper and remove the lining paper. Trim off the crisp sides of the cake, and roll up with the greaseproof paper inside the sponge. Place on a wire rack, with the join underneath, and leave to cool.

To make the filling, whisk the cream until it will stand in soft peaks and fold in the chopped strawberries. Unroll the cooled sponge and remove the greaseproof paper. Spread the filling evenly over the sponge and roll up again.

To make the sauce, put the strawberries and icing sugar into a blender or food processor and blend to a purée. Rub through a nylon sieve to remove the pips.

Cover each serving plate with some strawberry sauce, then put a slice of roulade in the centre. Place a few drops of cream on the sauce and drag a skewer through the sauce to make an attractive design.

SERVES 8

Nutritional content per serving: Carbohydrate: 43 Fat: 24 Fibre: 2 Kilocalories: 280

Pan-fried Apples

3 large Cox's Orange Pippin apples
1 tablespoon lemon juice
40 g (1½ oz) butter
2 tablespoons soft brown sugar
3 tablespoons Calvados or brandy
2 tablespoons chopped hazelnuts, toasted

Peel and core the apples and slice into rings, then sprinkle with lemon juice to prevent them from turning brown.

Heat the butter in a pan until melted, then add the apples and sprinkle over the sugar. Cook gently for 4 minutes, turning once, until the apples are soft and tinged golden brown at the edges.

Remove from the heat, pour over the Calvados or brandy and stir until combined. Serve on warmed plates, sprinkle with the nuts and serve with cream or thick yogurt.

SERVES 4

Nutritional content per serving: Carbohydrate: 9 Fat: 11 Fibre: 1 Kilocalories: 160

Pan-fried Apples; Hazelnut and Strawberry Roulade (top); Strawberry Oat Sundae

STRAWBERRY OAT SUNDAE

50 g (2 oz) porridge oats
125 ml (4 fl oz) milk
2 teaspoons clear honey
4 tablespoons Greek yogurt
2 tablespoons Cointreau
125 g (4 oz) strawberries, sliced
1 peach, stoned and sliced
2 tablespoons flaked almonds, toasted

Put the oats, milk and honey into a bowl, mix together and leave to soak for 15 minutes.

Fold in the yogurt and Cointreau with the fruits reserving 4 strawberry slices for decoration, and mix together carefully.

Spoon into glass dishes, sprinkle with the almonds and decorate with the reserved strawberry slices.

SERVES 4

Nutritional content per serving: Carbohydrate: 18 Fat: 9 Fibre: 3 Kilocalories: 180

Feuilleté normande

500 g (1 lb) Cox's Orange Pippins, peeled, cored and sliced
2 tablespoons clear honey
1 teaspoon mixed spice
1 teaspoon cinnamon
3 cloves
25 g (1 oz) sultanas
25 g (1 oz) raisins
300 g (10 oz) frozen puff pastry, defrosted
1 tablespoon caster sugar
1 tablespoon chopped hazelnuts
4 tablespoons whipped cream or thick yogurt to serve

Put the apples, honey, spices and cloves into a heavy-based pan, cover and cook gently for 15 minutes until softened, stirring occasionally. Add the sultanas and raisins, cover and leave to cool.

Divide the pastry into 6 pieces, then roll out thinly into 12 cm (5 inch) squares and trim the edges.

Put a spoonful of filling into the centre of each square and fold over the corners to resemble an envelope. Brush with water, sprinkle with the sugar and nuts, then place on a baking sheet and chill for 20 minutes.

Bake in a preheated oven, 200°C, 400°F, Gas Mark 6 for 25–30 minutes until crisp and golden.

Serve either with a spoonful of whipped cream or thick yogurt in the centre.

Freezing: is recommended. Before cooking, open freeze, then put into a polythene bag, seal and return to the freezer. These will keep for up to 3 months. Cook from frozen for 30–35 minutes.

SERVES 6

Nutritional content per serving: Carbohydrate: 58 Fat: 24 Fibre: 5 Kilocalories: 300

Lychee and apricot compôte

Use Hunza apricots if you can find them – they are delicious baby apricots from the Hunza Valley in northern India. They are much sweeter than ordinary dried apricots, so you may need to add a little lemon juice; they also retain their stones. They are the natural brown colour, as they have not been sprayed with sulphur dioxide

1 x 425 g (15 oz) can lychees
175 g (6 oz) dried or Hunza apricots
2 large oranges
2 tablespoons pine kernels, toasted

Drain the lychees and make the liquid up to 300 ml (½ pint). Put the apricots into a saucepan, pour over the liquid, cover and bring to the boil. Turn off the heat and leave to soak for 1 hour. Bring to the boil again, covered, simmer gently for 10 minutes and leave to cool. Turn into a glass bowl with the lychees.

Pare off thin strips of orange rind with a potato peeler and cut into needle-fine shreds. Blanch in boiling water for 1 minute, then drain and dry on kitchen paper.

Peel the oranges with a serrated-edge knife and cut into segments, removing all the membrane. Add to the bowl and mix together gently.

Sprinkle with pine kernels and orange rind and serve chilled.

SERVES 6

Nutritional content per serving: Carbohydrate: 28 Fat: 3 Fibre: 12 Kilocalories: 150

Bananas with Rum

25 g (1 oz) unsalted butter
25 g (1 oz) soft brown sugar
4 bananas, halved lengthways
2 tablespoons rum

Heat the butter in a frying pan until melted then stir in the sugar. Add the bananas to the pan and cook gently for 3 minutes, turning once.

Arrange the bananas on a warmed serving dish and spoon over the juices.

Warm the rum in a ladle, ignite and pour over the bananas. Serve flaming, with cream.

SERVES 4

Nutritional content per serving: Carbohydrate: 35 Fat: 6 Fibre: 5 Kilocalories: 205

Feuilleté Normande; Lychee and Apricot Compôte (bottom); Bananas with Rum

Almond and Apricot Tart

ALMOND PASTRY:
175 g (6 oz) plain flour
75 g (3 oz) butter or margarine
50 g (2 oz) ground almonds
2 tablespoons caster sugar
1 egg yolk
1–2 tablespoons water
FILLING:
175 g (6 oz) dried apricots, soaked overnight
300 ml (½ pint) water
50 g (2 oz) soft brown sugar
1 egg
50 g (2 oz) margarine
125 g (4 oz) ground almonds
a few drops almond flavouring
50 g (2 oz) flaked almonds
2 tablespoons apricot brandy
icing sugar, sieved, for dusting

To make the pastry, sift the flour into a bowl and rub in the butter or margarine until the mixture resembles breadcrumbs, then stir in the ground almonds and sugar. Add the egg yolk and enough water to mix to a firm dough. Turn on to a floured surface and knead lightly until smooth, then chill for 20 minutes.

Roll the pastry out thinly on a floured surface and use to line a 20 cm (8 inch) flan ring, placed on a baking sheet. Chill again for a further 30 minutes.

To make the filling, cook the apricots in the water for 10 minutes then drain well, reserving the liquid, and chop the apricots. Place the sugar, egg, margarine, ground almonds and flavouring in a bowl and beat well until smooth. Place half the apricots in the flan case and spoon the almond mixture over the top. Smooth the top with a palette knife and sprinkle over the flaked almonds.

Bake in a preheated oven, 200°C, 400°F, Gas Mark 6 for 15 minutes, then reduce the temperature to 190°C, 375°F, Gas Mark 5 and bake for 15–20 minutes until firm and golden brown.

To make the sauce, place the remaining apricots in a blender or food processor with 6 tablespoons of the reserved liquid and the apricot brandy and blend until smooth.

Remove the flan from the tin, sprinkle with icing sugar and serve in slices surrounded with sauce.

SERVES 8

Nutritional content per serving: Carbohydrate: 40 Fat: 29 Fibre: 10 Kilocalories: 450

Apple and Hazelnut Strudel

500 g (1 lb) dessert apples, peeled, cored and chopped
50 g (2 oz) soft brown sugar
50 g (2 oz) sultanas
1 teaspoon ground cinnamon
½ teaspoon grated nutmeg
3 sheets filo pastry
40 g (1½ oz) butter, melted
125 g (4 oz) hazelnuts, chopped finely and toasted
icing sugar, sieved, for dusting

Put the apples into a bowl with the sugar, sultanas and spices and mix together until well coated. Lay a sheet of filo pastry on a work surface and brush with melted butter. Repeat with 2 further sheets of pastry, then sprinkle on all but 2 tablespoons of the hazelnuts. Turn the apple mixture on to the pastry and spread evenly, leaving a 5 cm (2 inch) border on each long side.

Roll the pastry up from one of the long sides and place on a baking sheet. Brush with butter and sprinkle with the remaining nuts. Bake in a preheated oven, 190°C, 375°F, Gas Mark 5 for 30 minutes until golden brown. Sprinkle with icing sugar and serve while warm.

SERVES 6

Nutritional content per serving: Carbohydrate: 30 Fat: 13 Fibre: 4 Kilocalories: 240

Almond and Apricot Tart; Apple and Hazelnut Strudel (bottom); Fresh Figs with Raspberry Sorbet

FRESH FIGS WITH RASPBERRY SORBET

FRESH FIGS, WITH THEIR LUSCIOUS SOFT PINK FLESH, ARE ENTIRELY EDIBLE AND DO NOT NEED TO BE PEELED

500 g (1 lb) raspberries
125 g (4 oz) caster sugar
300 ml (½ pint) water
1 egg white
8 ripe figs
mint or geranium leaves to decorate

To make the sorbet, put the raspberries into a blender or food processor and blend until smooth. Rub through a sieve to remove the pips.

Put the sugar and water into a saucepan and heat gently until the sugar has dissolved, then boil for 5 minutes. Add the raspberry purée and leave to cool.

Pour into a rigid, freezerproof container, cover, seal and freeze for about 4 hours until half frozen.

Whisk the egg white until stiff, put into the blender or food processor with the half-frozen purée, and blend until well mixed. Return to the container, cover, seal and freeze until firm.

Make a deep cross cut in the top of each fig and open out slightly. Scoop some sorbet into the centre of each fig and arrange 2 figs on each serving plate. Decorate with mint or geranium leaves.

SERVES 4

Nutritional content per serving: Carbohydrate: 44 Fibre: 10 Kilocalories: 180

Gooseberry Tulips

The biscuit mixture makes about 10 tulips, 6 of which can be frozen for future use. Only put 3 biscuits on 1 baking sheet so that you don't have to mould too many at once

BISCUIT MIXTURE:
25 g (1 oz) plain flour, sifted
50 g (2 oz) caster sugar
1 egg white
25 g (1 oz) butter, melted
FILLING:
500 g (1 lb) gooseberries
125 g (4 oz) caster sugar
3 heads elderflower (optional)
300 ml (1/2 pint) double cream, whipped
fresh edible leaves to decorate

To make the tulips, put the flour and sugar into a bowl and make a well in the centre. Add the egg white and butter and beat until smooth.

Put 3 dessertspoonfuls of the mixture on to a greased and floured baking sheet and spread out thinly into 12 cm (5 inch) rounds. Bake, one baking sheet at a time, in a preheated oven, 200°C, 400°F, Gas Mark 6 for 6–7 minutes until golden at the edges.

Leave to cool slightly then remove from the baking sheet with a palette knife and place each one, top side downwards, over the base of a small tumbler. Mould the biscuit with your fingers to give wavy edges. Leave to harden, then remove carefully. Repeat with the remaining mixture and biscuits as they cook.

To make the filling, place the gooseberries and sugar in a pan with the elderflower tied in muslin, if using. Cover the pan and cook gently for 15 minutes until the gooseberries are soft.

Leave to cool slightly, remove the elderflower heads and purée the gooseberries in a blender or food processor.

Sieve to remove the tops and tails, then fold in the cream.

Spoon the filling into the biscuit tulips, decorate with the leaves and serve immediately.

Freezing: is recommended for the tulips. Pack very carefully with tissue in a rigid, freezerproof container, cover, seal and freeze. These will keep for up to 3 months. To defrost, unpack and leave at room temperature for 5 minutes.

SERVES 4

Nutritional content per serving: Carbohydrate: 48 Fat: 38 Fibre: 8 Kilocalories: 535

Peach Brulée

1 peach, peeled, stoned and sliced
1 tablespoon apricot brandy
150 g (5 oz) double cream
150 ml (1/4 pint) Greek yogurt
15 g (1/2 oz) soft brown sugar
peach slices to decorate

Divide the peach slices between 4 glasses. Pour liqueur into each one.

Whisk the cream until it stands in soft peaks, then fold in the yogurt. Spoon over the peaches to cover completely, then sprinkle the sugar all over the surface.

Chill for 1 hour and allow the sugar to dissolve before serving, decorated with peach slices.

SERVES 4

Nutritional content per serving: Carbohydrate: 9 Fat: 26 Kilocalories: 275

Gooseberry Tulips; Peach Brulée (bottom), Forest Fruit Ice Cream in an Ice Bowl (see recipe overleaf)

Forest fruit ice cream in an ice bowl

YOU WILL NEED 3 GLASS OR PLASTIC BOWLS OF 21 CM (8½ INCH), 20 CM (8 INCH) and 15 CM (6 INCH) DIAMETERS TO MAKE THE ICE BOWL. IT IS VERY EASY TO MAKE, BUT NEEDS PATIENCE IF YOU WANT A DECORATED BOWL. IT WILL LAST FOR ABOUT 30 MINUTES BEFORE IT VERY GRADUALLY STARTS TO MELT

125 g (4 oz) redcurrants
125 g (4 oz) blackcurrants
2 tablespoons sugar
50 ml [2 fl oz) water
250 g (8 oz) raspberries
2 egg whites
125 g (4 oz) caster sugar
300 ml (½ pint) double cream
TO DECORATE:
8 strawberries, sliced
2 redcurrant sprigs
strawberry leaves

Put the redcurrants and blackcurrants into a pan with the sugar and water, cover and cook over a gentle heat for 10 minutes until soft. Put into a blender or food processor with the raspberries and blend to a purée. Sieve to remove the pips and leave to cool completely.

Whisk the egg whites until stiff, then gradually whisk in the caster sugar. Fold the fruit purée into the cream, then fold in the egg whites until thoroughly mixed. Turn into a rigid, freezerproof container, cover, seal and freeze until solid.

To make the ice bowl, pour 150 ml (¼ pint) water into the largest bowl and freeze until solid. Pour a further 450 ml (¾ pint) water into the same bowl, place the medium bowl inside and fill it with weights to keep it in position; the water will rise to the top. Use sticky tape to keep the medium bowl well centred. Freeze until solid.

Loosen the inner bowl by pouring hot water into it and swirling it round, then remove it.

Dip the strawberry slices and leaves into water and arrange them on the ice at the side of the bowl, then freeze again for 30 minutes. Pour in about 750 ml (1¼ pints) water, place the smallest bowl inside, weigh down and centralize as before and freeze overnight until solid.

To loosen the ice bowl, pour in hot water and swirl it around, as before, then remove the small bowl. Dip the large bowl into hot water to loosen, then take out the ice bowl and return to the freezer until required.

Transfer the ice cream to the refrigerator 30 minutes before serving to soften. Place the ice bowl on a lipped plate to contain the water as it melts, scoop the ice cream into the centre and decorate with redcurrant sprigs and strawberry leaves.

SERVES 8

Nutritional content per serving: Carbohydrate: 25 Fat: 18 Fibre: 5 Kilocalories: 260

INDEX

ACKNOWLEDGEMENTS

Series Editor: **Nicola Hill**
Sub Editor: **Sophy Roberts**
Art Director: **Sara Kidd**
Designer: **Sue Storey**
Production Controller: **Alyssum Ross**
Photographer: **Roger Stowell**
Home Economist: **Carole Handslip**
Stylist: **Marian Price**
Jacket Photographer: **Vernon Morgan**